THE GREATEST DAY OF MY LIFE

—a human interest memoir of a 92-year-old World War II veteran and his diverse careers

THE GREATEST DAY OF MY LIFE

—a human interest memoir of a 92-year-old World War II veteran and his diverse careers

By Leonard Finz

The Greatest Day of My Life

Copyright © 2017 Leonard L. Finz

Published by:

Lifetime Press, Inc.
410 E. Jericho Turnpike
Mineola, NY 11501
516-592-6040

Printed in the United States of America

ISBN: 978-0-9833534-4-7

DEDICATION

In memory of Pearl, my beloved wife of 67 years, my love, my best friend, my career partner throughout her life – and beyond.

1952
With Pearl at the Stork Club in Shreveport, LA
where I was the featured performer in the show.

1954
With Pearl in Cape Cod, MA
where I was the featured performer in a supper club.

2014
With Pearl on December 26, 2014
celebrating our 66th wedding anniversary.

MY DIVERSE CAREERS

- Soldier

- Musician

- Entertainer

- Politician

- Judge

- Trial Lawyer

- Author

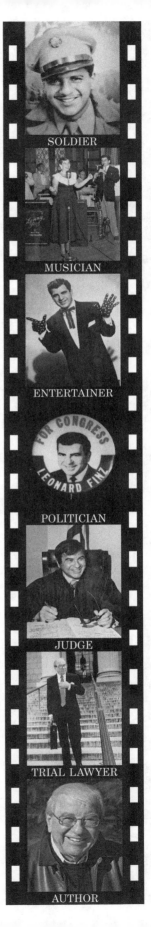

SOLDIER

MUSICIAN

ENTERTAINER

POLITICIAN

JUDGE

TRIAL LAWYER

AUTHOR

INTRODUCTION

Given my age and its vagaries, the time has come to record some of the meaningful events of my rather divergent life. For this purpose, I omit such priceless moments as my wonderful marriage of almost 68 years that ended in May of 2016 with the passing of my beloved and cherished wife, the births of my precious daughter, a retired nurse, and devoted son, a prominent lawyer, their spouses, both lawyers, and my loving grandchildren, all of whom are law school graduates. I do, however, include a very brief note about my family.

More than 16 million men and women served our country in World War II. In this, the year 2017, released statistics show that there are fewer than 5% remaining survivors. Losing World War II veterans at the rate of 500 each day, and rising with each passing month, it is estimated that by the end of 2018 there will be less than 1% of surviving World War II veterans. It is a staggering statistic with no predictor as to whether I will be counted within that infinitesimal group.

Thus, time being of the essence, what I have written here is a composite of many deep emotions and wondrous experiences that describe some of the challenging highlights of my life. These are my own words, the words of a 92-year-old warrior who believes that it is still the human-interest story that not only captures the day, but lives on far beyond it. To that end, I trust I will have satisfied this most demanding component to the content that follows.

Now, to my memoir...

THE LOWER EAST SIDE OF MANHATTAN

I was born in 1924, in a fourth-floor walk-up tenement on the Lower East Side of Manhattan, delivered not by a doctor in a hospital, but by a midwife in a small apartment. Rivington Street, where the building was located, was one of the immigrant melting pots surrounded by Delancey, Orchard, and Allen streets. Push carts and street vendors were everywhere,

shouting out their wares in voices loud enough to be heard through the open windows of our small two-bedroom apartment shared with my immigrant parents who came from Turkey, my two older brothers, and older sister. Moving out to Brooklyn when I was three years old, I would return every Sunday with my father who visited his mother (my grandmother) who lived in a one-bedroom apartment. He would place a few dollars in her wrinkled and arthritic hands with each visit. With one bathroom on the floor to be shared by six other families (similar to our own living conditions when we lived in that tenement building), I still have the jolting memories of the smells and ugliness everyone must have suffered. Although the tenements served as a first home to those immigrants such as my parents who passed legally through Ellis Island, they were disgusting places where human comfort and dignity were nowhere to be found.

A PLACE CALLED BROOKLYN

The move to Brooklyn was a huge step up since my father Samuel, who was self-taught in English, got a job with the Metropolitan Life Insurance Company as a "debit man". His role was to collect the two to three dollar a month premiums from those who purchased small life insurance policies. He would keep a hand-written record and visit the clients of Metropolitan Life in their apartments, where after a while he would be treated like a member of the family. For an immigrant to be so employed in such a responsible and demanding role by a premier company was indeed a testament to my father's honesty, integrity, and ability to integrate so quickly into the American culture.

"YOUR NAME 'LAZER' SOUNDS TOO FOREIGN"

I started elementary school at P.S. 226 located on 60th Street and 23rd Avenue in the Bensonhurst section of Brooklyn. I was in the third grade when something happened that has had an effect upon my entire life to this day. Here it is...

When my mother took me to school to enroll me as a first-grade student, she gave my name to the teacher as "Eleazer", although it was set out erroneously in my birth certificate as "Leazer". I had been named in honor of my grandfather, Eleazer, a biblical name described in the Old Testament with reverence. The teacher doing the paper work, and unfamiliar with the name, entered it as, "Lazer", which from that point on became the name listed on my official public school records.

One day when in the third grade, my teacher told me to remain in the classroom after the other children had left, saying there was something she wanted to discuss. Since I usually received an "A" or "B" for conduct, and was doing well enough in my subjects, I was filled with anxiety as to whether I had done something wrong. I was somewhat relieved when my teacher said everything was fine, but that she did have a message for me to take home to my parents.

In essence, she said that the name "Lazer" sounded much too foreign, and that my mother and father should change my name to one that sounded more American-like. It should be noted that this was the year 1932 when cultural sensitivities were not a great part of the American traditions we have honored for decades since. When I returned to our apartment (which was across the street from the school), I said nothing to my mother, waiting for my father to come home from work so that I could pass along the message given to me by my teacher to the two of them together. When he did arrive, I related what the teacher had said.

After some long discussion, my parents felt compelled to obey my teacher's "suggestion." Unsure of what the consequences would be if they refused, they finally came up with a name that to them at the time, had some euphonic resemblance to "Lazer". They settled on "Leonard". And it has been "Leonard" ever since, from that evening in 1932 to today, eighty-five years later. Of course, such a discriminatory and disrespectful act by a teacher today would probably cost him or her a teaching career.

MY ENTRY INTO THE WORLD OF MUSIC

I was all of eight years of age when my parents, who loved music, (my mother Sarah loved the popular songs of the day and my father played the banjo and also loved opera) bought me a soprano saxophone for $50, the terms being $5 down, with the balance to be paid over a year. He and my mother wanted me to become involved in music since I had shown early signs of some singing and musical talent.

In fact, I would often sing solo in the school assembly and my teachers would always call upon me to perform at class functions. Although we were in the middle of the Great Depression and money was scarce, my parents nevertheless sacrificed, and started me on music lessons at fifty cents for a half hour (real money in those days) at the New York School of Music.

A year later, my parents hired a private sax teacher for lessons at even a higher cost. I had to practice more than an hour each day and pity me if I didn't. In fact, the very first words uttered by my father when he would come home from work would be, "Did you practice today?" It would always be followed up with, "How long?" There was a practice discipline in place that I could never ignore. He was equally rigid with my older sister Mollie, for whom piano lessons had been arranged as well. But in addition to music, my father loved poetry. A night would not pass when my mother,

3

brothers, sister, and I would be gathered together as my father would read passages from his favorite poet, Henry Wadsworth Longfellow.

Back to my soprano sax... It had the look of an alto sax, but was half its size. A rarity, it would probably be worth thousands today. Within three years however, we traded it in for a Buescher alto saxophone, which I still have to this day. And it was my ability to read music (credit the years of lessons I had taken) and play an alto sax (with a solid musical tone) that lead to my being the youngest musician ever invited to join the Lowe's Cadet Band, a fifty-piece regional orchestra. I was decked out in a fancy uniform, playing at community concerts and special patriotic functions, all at 12 years of age.

Indeed, as I look back in time, although I developed into a trained musician, ridding myself of the soprano sax and replacing it with an alto was not one of the greatest days of my life.

THE HIGH SCHOOL OF MUSIC AND ART

In the eighth grade, and about to complete elementary school, I was ready to enroll into Lafayette High School, no more than fifteen minutes from where I lived. Changes came however, when my music teacher insisted I apply to the High School of Music and Art (commonly called HSMA) in upper Manhattan. In existence for only one year, it was the special pride of Mayor Fiorello H. La Guardia. He wanted a specialized high school for children gifted in either music or art. But acceptance as a music student required a rigid audition.

I remember carrying my alto sax in its case and making a two-hour trip through the subway system to the school. It was a long journey, particularly for my mother who accompanied me. When we arrived at what resembled an old Gothic castle on a steep hill, we found our way into a large auditorium and checked in. Within a half hour my name was called. Directed to the large stage, I suddenly faced the music director and other music teachers on the faculty. My alto sax was already out of its case and held by a strap around my neck. I was so nervous I thought I would throw up. With great relief however, I didn't. "Sit in the chair in front of the music stand," I was ordered by one of the faculty members. "Play any piece you want." With that, I played "Nola", a selection I had practiced many times, it being an assignment from my sax instructor. When finished, someone placed a sheet of music on the stand and said, "Play it." This was a test of my ability to sight-read music. The armpits of my shirt were already drenched with perspiration. In almost a state of panic, I played the sheet as best I could, praying I didn't screw it up.

To make matters even more difficult, another sheet of music was placed on the stand and I was told to sight-read it, not with sax this time, but with voice. Reading music was one thing. After all, I had been taking formal lessons since I was eight years old. Sight-reading by singing was quite another. I fumbled through having no clue whether I was on target or having missed by a country mile. "You'll hear from us one way or the other," a voice rang out. I couldn't get out of there fast enough, upset that my elementary school music teacher caused me to suffer such torture.

A week later, I received the news. "The High School of Music and Art has accepted you." Shock was followed by relief, followed by exhilaration. I couldn't believe I made it.

Although good news, it still didn't rise to being the greatest day of my life.

THE BIG BAND ERA AND MY HSMA SWING BAND

Being accepted into HSMA in upper Manhattan was quite an honor for me. The High School of Music and Art has since been moved to Lincoln Center in Manhattan, having merged with the School for the Performing Arts. Both are under the official umbrella of The Fiorello H. LaGuardia High School of Music & Art and Performing Arts. While I

spent almost four hours a day traveling from Brooklyn to HSMA on an incomplete subway system, it did however, have its unpredictable rewards. For example, to get to upper Manhattan, I had to take two local trains to 42nd street. With no connecting lines to the IRT or Independent Subway at the time, I would have to walk up two flights of stairs to the level above where I would then exit onto the street. As a result, I would have to walk to the subway that would take me to upper Manhattan each morning, and of necessity pass by the New York Paramount Theatre located in the Times Square area.

In those days (referring to the late 1930's), the theatre featured a first run movie that would start at 8 am, followed by a big live band and show. The ticket price at that hour was all of twenty-five cents. That's when I would cut class to see and hear my idols of the swing band era: Glen Miller, Benny Goodman, Tommy Dorsey, Jimmy Dorsey, Stan Kenton, Les Brown, Woody Herman, and a host of others who were the greats in the big band business during that very special period. Although I would cut class to sit in an almost empty theatre, I am grateful to this day that I did. Seeing and hearing the music legends of that era was an experience I have cherished for more than seventy-five years.

I cannot describe my HSMA life without including the following... Aside from being taught the clarinet by one of the finest classical clarinetist in the city, and later sitting in the first clarinetist chair of HSMA's outstanding symphony orchestra, I also became the leader of HSMA's prize-winning swing band. This came about since the leader had graduated and a replacement had to be found. The selection of a new leader of the HSMA's big jazz band was then put to a vote and I was elected unanimously. I felt extremely humbled by the action taken.

Fronting the orchestra that had five saxes, three trumpets, three trombones, piano, drums, guitar, and string bass, was a blast. We had the stock arrangements of the big bands, and my standing in front with clarinet in hand a la Benny Goodman and Artie Shaw, my two idols, are memories I carry to this day. But even all of that glory didn't make any particular day the greatest one of my life.

MY STEADY WEEKEND GIG IN A SMOKEY JOINT

I was 16 years old when as part of a trio with a piano player and drummer, I had a weekend job playing sax in a gin mill. The joint was located in that section of upper Manhattan known at the time as Italian Harlem. It had a small stage and dance floor to match. The pungent smell of cigarette smoke and beer was  enough to knock you over. I also remember the jukebox that would be played without stop during our breaks. The Tommy Dorsey record of Frank Sinatra, backed by the Pied Pipers, singing his blowout hit, "I'll Never Smile Again", would be played over and over again (at a nickel a pop). The bar and grill customers couldn't get enough of what would later become an iconic recording for all time. In fact, it is as much in my memory today as if it were played for the first time, just yesterday. And every time I hear Sinatra singing this classic on Sirius satellite radio, I can almost still smell stale cigarette smoke and beer that was such a rancid part of the room's dimly lit atmosphere.

As for the job, it was a steady music gig on Friday, Saturday, and Sunday from 9pm to 3am, for which I earned $3 a night. My non-musician friends were earning less than that working for nickel and dime tips delivering pharmacy prescriptions. My mother, as loving and caring as she always was, would be waiting up for me in the kitchen until she saw that I arrived home safely. I would be upset that it was four o'clock in the morning and she shouldn't be up so late. But being the wonderful mother she was, she would smile in her loving way, kiss me goodnight, and only then would she go to sleep.

As for my weekend music jobs in that smoke-filled bar and grill, although they added to my overall band experience, they had little effect upon the greatest day of my life.

MY GREAT JAZZ TRUMPET PLAYER SHORTY ROGERS

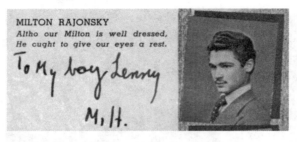

MILTON RAJONSKY
*Altho our Milton is well dressed,
He ought to give our eyes a rest.*

To My boy Lenny
M. H.

All of the guys in my HSMA swing band were outstanding musicians, but several made it real big in Hollywood. First, there was Milton Rajonsky, who later took on the name, "Shorty Rogers". He was an extremely talented jazz trumpet player. Upon graduation from HSMA, his unique talent was quickly noticed by Woody Herman and Stan Kenton, two of the biggest names during the big band era. Featured on the trumpet and flugelhorn with the Kenton and Herman orchestras, he quickly developed the rep as the West coast's most talented trumpet jazz-man. Signed up with RCA Victor and Atlantic records, his albums to this day are legendary. Within a short time, his many talents as a jazz artist and arranger came to the attention of famous Hollywood film producers. Consequently, Shorty wrote and arranged the background music for more than thirty Hollywood films. Unfortunately, he died of cancer at the age of 70, but his great musical artistry continues to live on.

MY GREAT JAZZ PIANIST HAL SCHAEFER

The other big name in my HSMA swing band, was Hal Schaefer, a remarkable jazz pianist. Shortly after graduating from HSMA, his enormous talent was discovered by Duke Ellington. The Duke took great pride in stating that Hal's

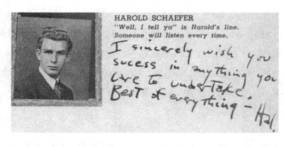

HAROLD SCHAEFER
*"Well, I tell ya" is Harold's line.
Someone will listen every time.*

I sincerely wish you
sucess in anything you
are to undertake.
Best of everything - Hal.

fingers on the keyboard were so fast that he ranked him right up there with Art Tatum, the number one piano jazz artist at the time. Putting his piano artistry on hold, Hal became a vocal coach to a number of Hollywood stars. These are some of the big-time celebrities he coached: Judy Garland, Barbra Streisand, Mitzi Gaynor, Robert Wagner, Jane Russell, Marilyn Monroe, and the list goes on. In fact, Marilyn's singing voice in, "Gentlemen Prefer Blondes", the Hollywood mega hit, was singularly tutored by Hal as her personal vocal coach.

On the human interest and sensational side, Marilyn and Hal had a love affair shortly after her divorce from Joe DiMaggio—a marriage that lasted only nine months. DiMaggio was convinced that the Marilyn and Hal relationship was the root of the breakup, and having a strong jealous nature, he even hired private detectives after the divorce to spy on Marilyn and Hal. On one occasion that made national news, DiMaggio was tipped off that Marilyn and Hal were in a certain house together. Sneaking onto the property, DiMaggio, a friend, and two hired goons then broke down the back door expecting to surprise Marilyn and Hal in a love tryst. As it was, they smashed the door of the wrong house, and the occupant, a middle-aged woman, reacted hysterically, as if she was being assaulted. Hearing the loud noises, and suspecting that they were being secretly spied upon, Marilyn and Hal fled from the house they were in which was next door, and out of the grasp of DiMaggio, his friend, and the goon squad. Interestingly enough, DiMaggio's friend turned out to be none other than Mr. Blue eyes himself, Frank Sinatra.

Writing his memoir years later, Hal stated if they had crashed the right door of the house occupied by Marilyn and Hal at the time, he probably would have wound up as dog meat. After that close encounter with disaster, and after receiving many death threats with warnings to stay away from her, Hal never saw or spoke to Marilyn Monroe again.

A HOLLYWOOD OFFER I DID REFUSE

After the war, in the early 1950s, when Hal Schaefer was riding high with the celebrity elite of Hollywood, I telephoned him one day. After all, he was my jazz pianist with my HSMA swing band from 1939 to 1942 and now a real biggie with the Hollywood in-crowd. The reason for my call was  to tell him I had just read a flattering article and wished to congratulate him upon his success. Happy to hear from me, he urged, "Come on out to the coast Lenny. You'll be back in show business, big time." But timing is everything in life. I had a beautiful wife who I loved, a young daughter I cherished, and another career that needed to get started. I wasn't about to dislodge my family, pack everyone up, and try to hook up with the

Hollywood crazies on the fly. Although I knew Hal was serious and not just making small talk, it was a risk I couldn't subject my family to at that time. Perhaps, as the clichéd expression goes, "I could have been a star." But as I look back, I have no regrets. Sadly, Hal died in 2012, having relocated permanently to Ft. Lauderdale, Florida, shortly after the Marilyn Monroe debacle and his close encounter with a potentially lethal outcome.

MY 1942 HSMA YEAR BOOK

LEONARD FINZ
"Out of the gloom a ship came to rest."
With Leonard's swing band one of the best.

From time to time I browse through the pages of my 1942 HSMA Yearbook and view the photos of Shorty and Hal while nostalgically reading their hand-written messages next to their photos. In his typically cool manner, Shorty (his first name was really "Milton") wrote simply: "To my boy Lenny! —Milt." As for Hal, his message was more formal: "I sincerely wish you success in anything you undertake. Best of Everything —Hal." I even check out my own photo, and am still surprised to see me with a full head of thick, jet-black hair, moustache and all. I have always felt a special pride at what the editors wrote in their two-line printed description next to my photo: "Out of the gloom a ship came to rest. With Leonard's swing band one of the best."

My classmates were convinced that when I got out of HSMA I would be fronting and leading a top jazz band professionally. They would constantly heap praise upon me. And coming from many of the most gifted and talented young musicians in New York City, was indeed most rewarding. These are a few comments hand written in my yearbook by some of them: "Whose bands are you going to put out when you get to the top?"; "I'll see you on the stage of the Paramount"; "To a handsome bloke with a Maestro's stroke"; "To a darn good swing band leader"; "What would HSMA be without Maestro Finz?"; "Loads of luck Maestro"; "To dear Maestro Finz— may you always have success"; "A great musician"; "A swell leader"; "Hey Maestro—be hearing you on the radio"; "We enjoyed your music for four years"; "To dear Maestro Finz—may you always have success"; "A future Guy Lombardo"; "Keep 'em swinging"; "May bigger audiences be yours"; "To the future Vaughn Monroe"; "Music in your veins"; "To a very grand musician"; "We appreciate your swell band"; "To a fellow with rhythm and personality"; "Music Maestro Please." And more...

Plus, under a special column in the year book, titled: "WE LEAVE IT", the thrust of which named ten teachers at HSMA followed by a few words setting out what was being left to them upon our graduation, there was only one student in our entire class who alone was named: "To Mr. Weiss (he was the faculty advisor of the swing band) hot jazz galore, another Finz to take the floor. The original can't stay." And under another special column titled: "IT'S IN THE STARS", the following: "With music by genial Maestro Finz, we see the Persian room." It was located in the world-famous Plaza Hotel, and the most elite and upscale showroom in Manhattan at the time.

What was most poignant (and most relevant even to this day 75 years later), is the printed message of HSMA's principal, Benjamin M. Steigman, PhD. These are a few excerpts: "... Ever since you came here to Music and Art your education has been set to the accompaniment of the guns of war. Term after term you have followed... the German invasion and conquest of fourteen independent nations... We hope the world in which you will live as men and women will not be a world in which looking pleasant is a pose to be commended for special occasions." How prophetic.

As to other notables at HSMA, there was Bess Meyerson (class of 1941), the former Miss America; my class mates, Bernie Garfield, first bassoonist with the New York Philharmonic and Philadelphia Orchestra, Ira Stadlen, who changed his name to Alan Swift. He played "Popeye" for several years on a network TV show, and was known in Hollywood as "the man with a thousand voices." His son who bears the name Lewis J. Stadlen, is a Broadway star who played the lead role of Groucho Marx in the hit Broadway musical, "Groucho", in addition to many other showbiz credits.

Some of the other notables who graduated from HSMA in later years are: Hal Linden, actor and Tony Award winner; Steven Botchco, producer of "L.A. Law", "Hill Street Blues", "NYPD Blue", and other TV blockbusters; Sean Daniel, producer of dozens of winning Hollywood films; James Burrows, of "Cheers" and other hit TV show fame; Peter Hyams, famed Hollywood producer and director of many hit movies; and the list of other famous HSMA graduates goes on...

As for my HSMA principal, teachers, the famous and celebrity classmates are all gone, and their passing does not make for some of the happier days of my life.

I was born August 17, 1924 in a tenement building on Rivington Street on the lower East Side of Manhattan.

With my older sister, my older brothers, and my mother
in front of our apartment in Brooklyn.
I am at the lower left, and age 4.

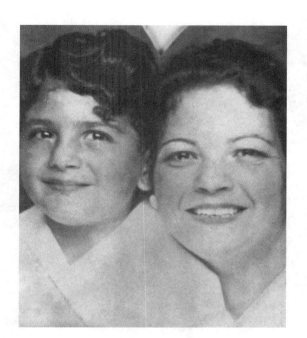

With my mother. I am 8 years old.

I am 10 years old.

This is a typical soprano saxophone (now a rarity). I started formal music lessons on this type of sax at age 8.

With other members of the Lowe's Cadet Band. At age 12, I was the youngest member of the 50 piece community band. I am in the first row and in the circle.

I am at age 13 with my Alto Saxophone, upon graduation from elementary school. I auditioned and was accepted at the High School of Music and Art.

My graduation Senior Souvenir (graduation) book.

This is an art student's depiction of HSMA.

This shows the Gothic architecture of the High School of Music and Art
in Upper Manhattan, commonly called HSMA, "The Castle on the Hill."

This is a candid photo taken in my math class. I am 16 years old, and on the right. 1940.

Board of Education
of the City of New York

High School of Music and Art

This Diploma is awarded to

Leonard Finz

who has satisfactorily completed the

Academic Course of Four Years and Major Music

and by proficiency in scholarship and by integrity of character
has merited graduation   January 1942

President Board of Education   Superintendent of Schools

Principal

My High School of Music and Art diploma. 1942.

My graduation from
the High School of Music and Art
wearing cap and gown. 1942.

We Leave It

♦♦♦

To Mrs. Muller, a scheduled day,
    each minute listed, all the way;
To Dennis, our indoor aviator,
    A Liquamatic elevator;
All this without delay,
Miss Horowitz gets thirty guys
    to send on forays for supplies;
A. Valenstein, a full eleven
    feet of space in 557;
To Mr. Weiss, hot jazz galore,
    another Finz to take the floor—
    The original can't stay;
To Mr. Cobb, some alchemy,
    to make a room for our aud b;
For Mrs. Schoenberg there is slated
    a senior book, prefabricated;
Miss Coleman gets all kinds of glues
    for mounting H. S. M. A. news
In scrapbooks every day;
Miss Allen, a fourth term class so bright
    it knows "d'Artanyun" isn't right;
To Mr. Cooper, cops to lurk
    and bar all flowers from where he'll work;
And to Mr. Sayers a register,
    wherein this Will he may inter.
    Executors, obey!

Written by   Janet Rumely

One of the entries in the Senior Souvenir book.

It's in the Stars

Another entry in the Senior Souvenir book.

Astrologers gaze at the heavens,
    the future to foresee
With Taurus, Aries and Leo.
    They state their prophecy:

"Rumely, the scientist,
    who digs in far-off lands
Takes famous photog Arnold there
    to snap the scenic sands
NEW YORKER'S young Art Editor,
    Liptak is hard at work,
Discussing a sketch of Comedian Brown
    who's profitably berserk!
Blanche Udren, famous journalist,
    in her story makes this claim,
'Enid, photographers' well-known model,
    is on her way to fame.'
Miss Janet Berger, a second Jane Ace,
    is popular on the air,
Stadlen pens her cleverscripts,
    for which he has a flair.
With music by genial Maestro Finz,
    we see the Persian Room;
Over there is Playboy Silver,
    who made his money in The Boom!
The rival of Cesar Romero's Nick N.,
    the Hollywood star,
His fast-talking press-agent Berger
    helped build him up on a 'bar'."

The stars are fading fast
    into a slightly clouded state.
Thank you Libra, Virgo, and Cancer,
    for a revealing glimpse of Fate!

I am on a weekend pass from Camp Pendleton, Virginia, during WWII. 1943.

With some of my army buddies after basic training at Camp Pendleton, Virginia. I am in the circle. 1943.

PVT. LENNY FINZ

Pvt. Lenny Finz Born Of Talent

By Cpl. Morton Diamond

"Talent on Parade," highly successful Fordsmen show, today, is proud to give, for your reading pleasure, the biography of a new camp entertainment star, Pvt. Leonard Finz. Not until just a few weeks ago, almost overnite, did Lenny emerge from the ordinary life of a private (KP, RSO detail, and Co.), into a camp celebrity.

Though young in years (Lenny celebrated his nineteenth birthday only last week), Pvt. Finz is a seasoned actor, musician, and director of shows. Let's look into Len's short but rich past.

Our young maestro was surrounded at home by a highly talented family; his dad played the banjo, his sister the piano, his brother the violin, and his mother sang. And so, it is not at all surprising that Leonard, the boy, became very much interested in music and singing. He procurred a saxophone and began knocking off those hot licks that have made him the popular saxman he is today.

Lenny's days of acting and entertaining go back to his elementary school days where he was quite a char-actor. At the ripe old age age of 10, he was already an established professional solo and choir singer. After completion of his elementary schooling, he received a scholarship to the High School of Music and Art in New York City. While attending the institution, Lenny played with various jazz bands in many big New York nite spots including the Waldorf-Astoria and McAlpin.

After completing extensive music courses in harmony, arranging and conducting, Pvt. Finz became the leader of the solid school swing band. Like Benny Goodman, beyond the realm of jazz, displayed his musical versatility by playing clarinet in the H.S.M.A. symphony orchestra. While with the organization, he composed and arranged clarinet quartets plus the lyrics and music to original ballads. Incidentally, he just sent in his latest composition, "A Soldier's Plea", to the contest sponsored by the War Dept. It really is a corker.

Not content with the prospect of a fine musical career before him, Lenny improved his ever-enlarging talents by taking up dramatics. Practical experience in this field was obtained in the "Borsht Circuit" (the Catskill Mts. of N. Y.), where he wrote and directed many shows at various well-known summer resorts.

The article in the G.I. Gazette, the camp army newspaper, after I was appointed Entertainment Director for the entire base. 1943.

With Joe Lewis, the heavy weight champion of the world who's appearance I arranged. We put on a show and "fought" three rounds in front of thousands of G.I.'s on the base. 1943.

20

I am composing music for the Camp Pendleton shows I put on each week for the G.I.'S as the camp entertainment director. 1943.

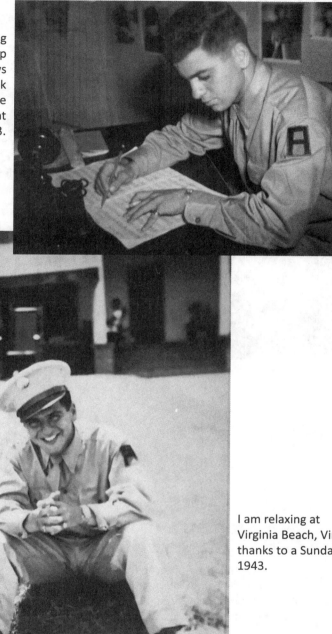

I am relaxing at Virginia Beach, Virginia, thanks to a Sunday pass. 1943.

With my buddies in the army following basic training. I am at the left in the bottom row. 1944.

I am saluting the American flag In Camp Pendleton, VA, during retreat (The American flag is brought down as the national anthem is played). 1943.

With my mom, dad, sister Mollie, on my first furlough
from Camp Pendleton, VA, during WWII. 1943.

Being a trained musician, I am transferred to the post's 272nd U.S. Army Band.
Although I was the lead alto in the sax section, I am playing clarinet
in one of Benny Goodman's big-band hit arrangements. 1944.

We are on the parade grounds playing a Sousa march for the troops marching in formation.
I am in the rear playing the clarinet, and in the circle. 1944.

The B.A. degree I received from NYU using the GI Bill of Rights
for my college education after I was discharged from the army. 1949.

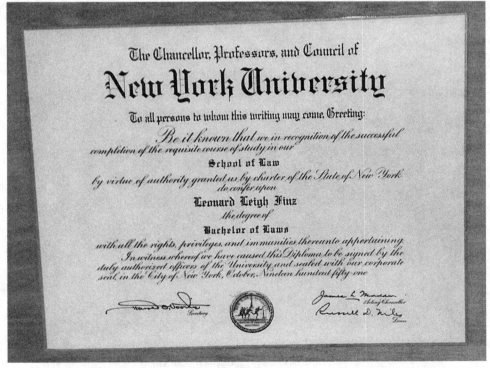

The L.L.B. (JD) degree I received from NYU using the GI Bill. 1951.

The Certificate of Merit certifying my election as President of the Pre-Bar Association of the
NYU School of Law. The Association covered the entire student body of the law school.
1950 – 1951.

The certificate certifying my membership to the Moot Court Board,
an honor society of the law school.
1950 – 1951.

THE 18-YEAR-OLD DRAFT AND WORLD WAR II

After four years of a rewarding music and academic education, I graduated from HSMA in January, 1942. Having completed high school, I started my own band in early 1942 and played for private parties in some of the finest hotels. To name a few: The Waldorf Astoria, The Hotel Pennsylvania, The McAlpin Hotel, The Astor Hotel, and a host of others. I was approaching 18-years-of-age and knew I would be called up by the first 18-year-old draft  ever enacted in the nation. I also knew I would soon be drafted without a guarantee that I would be assigned to an army band after basic training.

Having saved all I could from my music club-dates, I decided to spend it all on tuition for college. I had no doubt I would be drafted into the army but thought if I entered with at least one college semester behind me, my service assignment might be a more favorable one. With that goal in mind, I enrolled in NYU as a pre-med student with the hope I could continue my studies to become a doctor if I ever survived the war.

Every dollar I had ever saved (about $250, a fair sum at the time) all went toward my full tuition for the first semester I had to pay in advance (I took 16 credits at a cost of $18.00 a credit, plus books, etc.) But six weeks after I began, I received my 1A draft notice. Receiving it earlier than I expected, I had no choice but to withdraw from NYU without receiving any college credit at all.

When I went into the office of the Bursar (in charge of tuition) to request a partial refund of even $100, which in those days was big money, especially for me at the time, he surprisingly refused. I showed him my 1A draft notice telling him that the tuition I paid NYU in advance for a full semester was all the money I had saved up with a lot of hard work over a long period of time, and that my parents were not of the means to provide any financial assistance. He didn't budge. I pleaded with him that I had no choice, repeating that I had a 1A draft notice and would soon be ordered to report to the army of our nation at war. He sat there like a mindless statue and continued his refusal to grant me a partial refund. He just stared with cold indifference and a total lack of concern at an 18-year-old ready to sacrifice his life for his country.

It was a very hurtful experience but I learned much from the encounter. He either had discretion and refused to use it justifiably, or he was bound by an unjust rule that he as Bursar in a top executive position could have waived given the extreme compelling circumstances. In either case, it helped shape my own character so as never to be so unfeeling toward another human being in need and distress. Although unfortunate, I believe the sad encounter made me a better judge (my future role), and a better human being.

I was called up a short while after that, reported to 39 Whitehall Street in downtown Manhattan for a routine physical and was sworn into the army soon thereafter.

Transported by a military truck to Camp Upton in Yaphank, Long Island, I was outfitted with army clothing. It was early 1943 when I shipped out to Camp Pendleton, Virginia Beach, Virginia, and assigned to the 46th Coast Artillery for basic training. Four brutal months with Wilson, a Deep-South, bigoted, anti-Semite for a first sergeant, was my introduction to real army life. Having completed basic, most of the other draftees in my company were rewarded by receiving one stripe. With Wilson making the pick, I wasn't one of them. But then again, no big deal. Being promoted to private first class meant a big pay raise from $50 a month to $54. Although four dollars was real money, it would not change my life by not getting it, and I probably would have blown it in a crap game anyway.

MY INTRODUCTION TO A U.S. ARMY BAND

With basic training behind me, I sent home for my alto sax and clarinet. When the instruments arrived and I adlibbed familiar songs in my barracks, the guys in my platoon were floored. They were amazed that I could play whatever request they had and I was soon called the, "Barrack's Song Master". They also liked to attach a vowel to my last name and address me as "Finzi, the music guy from New York".

It was after my basic training when I introduced myself to some of the musicians assigned to the post's army band. In fact, I would sit in with the group at some of the dances they played since they liked my style and the sound of my horn. All fine musicians, they had been called into active duty when they were in the Pennsylvania 272nd U.S. Army Band Reserve. My playing sax and clarinet with the post band was a gift from heaven since they needed a lead alto in their swing band and an extra clarinet for their marching band. Although I loved sitting in with the guys who were more musician than soldier, my regular assignment remained with the 46th Coast Artillery. With that, I continued to be hassled by that redneck from Mississippi—First Sergeant Wilson.

Despite my joy in playing sax and clarinet with the 272nd Army Band, I was still under the claws of Wilson, who gave me every crap assignment in the book. My name would constantly appear on the posted roster for KP, latrine duty, guard duty, the cleaning out of coal furnaces, the scrubbing of the barrack's floor, and more. He took special pleasure in making my army life almost intolerable.

MY DEMERIT AND WEEKEND PASS

I had never forgotten how cruel and callous Sergeant Wilson was. This is a typical example... Our barracks had inspection every Saturday morning. Wilson, together with the platoon sergeant, and squad leader, would inspect each bunk and footlocker to see whether we complied with inspection rules. Every piece of equipment had to be in its right place, the blanket covering our bunk had to be tight enough to act like a spring if a dime was tossed on top of it, etc. Each soldier would be inspected as he stood at attention while Wilson checked out the shine on the shoes, the creases in the shirts, and so on. A missed cue would result in a demerit, which could cost you a weekend pass. It was Wilson who alone was the judge and jury and would decide the punishment to be imposed.

I was sixth down the line. All five G.I.'s ahead of me were already inspected and passed with no negatives reported. When Wilson reached me however, he ordered the platoon sergeant to give me a demerit because my "blanket is not tight enough." This was a lot of malarkey since I made certain that everything that Wilson would inspect was far above the standard called for, recognizing he would be focusing upon me more directly than upon the other guys in the barracks. Regarding the blanket not being "tight enough", it was tighter than a snare drum.

When I reported to the headquarters office after inspection in order to pickup my weekend pass, Wilson, with his usual smirk, said, "No pass. You failed inspection." I knew I couldn't reason or argue with him (it was a phony call), but I was now in a most difficult bind. Not having seen my mother since I entered the service, she had arranged a weekend visit to Virginia Beach. In fact, she was already on a bus to Norfolk, Virginia, there to take the three-hour ferry across Chesapeake Bay to Virginia Beach.

I informed Wilson of my mother's situation and pleaded with him to give me a pass. He still said, "No." Terribly upset, I responded, "Sergeant Wilson, please do this for me this one time. Give me any crap duty assignment you can dig up for me next week. Even double it, but don't do this to me now. My mother is already on her way and it's a twelve-hour trip. It's too late for me to call her off. "Please sergeant," I begged.

I could never forget or forgive his despicable response. In his typical southern drawl, and with a sickening smile that displayed his crooked teeth, he said, "Well now, isn't that... tough s**t," stretching out the last vulgar word.

Finally, I defied army rules and brought my grievances directly to our company's Executive Officer, Lt. Moore. He was an extremely decent gentleman whom I had gotten to know on a more personal basis as a result of my playing in the band at the officers' club dances. He was my cover and would protect me from Wilson whenever I was being driven too harshly. Of course, this didn't sit too well with my vindictive first sergeant, but somehow I had to protect myself from this regular army (those who made the military a career) bully. Lt. Moore summoned Wilson into his office. The door was then closed. After a few minutes, Wilson came out. This time his cynical smile was replaced by a sneer. Reluctantly, he issued me the weekend pass I should have received in the first place.

Before long, I was singing standards with the army swing band in the style of Dick Haymes and Frank Sinatra. As stated earlier, I always had a good singing voice (even at age five). My voice changed however, when I was

13 years old as maturity started to take over. High pitched soprano tones gave way to crackling deeper ones as adolescence arrived. Fortunately, my voice settled down when I hit 16, a transition that gave me a solid baritone sound. Still, even singing with the army band with all the pleasures that accompanied it, did not make for the best day of my life.

MY BEING ASSIGNED AS CAMP PENDELTON'S ENTERTAINMENT DIRECTOR

Soon after basic training, and after sitting in and playing dances at the officers' club, whatever talent I displayed came to the attention of the post's captain for special services. He needed an assistant to provide weekly entertainment to the thousands of soldiers stationed at Camp Pendleton. The captain explained that although the assignment would be a temporary one, the music, direction, and production of shows for the G.I.'s on the base would be under my complete control. Being only 18 years of age at the time provided me with an extraordinary experience. I recruited singers, comics, and musicians, putting on weekly shows for the thousands on the base. The productions were so well received that the army newspaper even gave me a front-

page story, photograph and all. The headline read, "Private Lenny Finz, Born of Talent." A storyline and bio followed which was as laudatory as any of today's entertainment critics who might write positively about a rock star.

As camp entertainment director, I arranged for the personal appearance of Joe Louis, the heavy weight boxing champion of the world. It was quite a move and overwhelmingly received by the thousands of Camp Pendleton's G.Is. This was especially so when I had a boxing ring erected on the parade grounds. The internationally famed Joe Louis and I planned and put on a three-round boxing match. In true show biz style, we had rehearsed each round. I recall the announcer (another G.I.) in the middle of the ring (as rehearsed) shouting out in a loud voice into a microphone, "And wearing black and white trunks, weighing 148 pounds, from Brooklyn, New York, who has never been in a boxing ring before... Private Lenny Finz." Polite applause followed. The announcer then went on, "And wearing red, white and blue trunks, weighing 212 pounds, the heavy-weight champion of the world... the one and only... Joe Louis." The thousands in attendance went wild. There were ear shattering shouts, screams, and whistles, the works! It was an eruption of sound that could be heard across the Atlantic.

As rehearsed, round one looked more like a track meet than a boxing match as I continued to run around the ring being chased by Joe. Round two was a duplicate of round one. And then came round three, the final round. Standing in front of the heavy weight champion with my fists only reaching up to his waist I lashed out with my right boxing glove pretending I had struck him hard on the left jaw. With that "blow" Joe Louis went down to the canvas like a bag of cement and was counted out for the full count. The troops loved it and so did Joe, whose sportsmanship and patriotism were always top drawer.

Although the whole production was a fantastic blast, it still was not the greatest day of my life.

USING MY G.I. BILL

Before I disclose the greatest day of my life, a few words about events and honors received after my World War II army discharge. Having only finished high school when I was drafted into the service in 1943, I used the G.I. bill to further my education. Since I was in the army for almost four years, I had much time to make up when the war was finally over. Toward that end, I started college in September 1946. Having taken maximum credits (sometimes twenty in a single semester) with full credits during the summer months, the accelerated programs paid off. From September 1946 to June of 1951, I had earned two degrees. One was a B.A. from NYU, the other an LLB (now a JD) from the NYU School of Law. In fact, in my senior year of law school, I was appointed to the Moot Court Board (a select debating society), and elected president of the Pre-Bar Association, the student body organization of the entire law school.

SHAME ON OUR NATION'S CAPITOL

There are many stories I can relate to my life in law school, but one particularly sticks out even to this day... As president, I was invited to the annual national law school conference held at a prominent hotel in Washington, D.C. I was also given the choice of selecting another student  officer to join me in representing our law school. I chose the vice-president of the Pre-Bar Association, one of the few black students in our senior class. He, my wife Pearl, and I drove to the nation's capital in my car. When we arrived at the hotel where the conference was to be held, we went directly to the front desk to check in having made prior reservations for two rooms. When my friend attempted to register, he was told, "This hotel does not accept Negros." I was outraged and demanded to speak to the manager. The nerdy twit who came to the desk and responded had the same racist message. It was a disgusting exhibition for my wife and me, but I knew it had to be a humiliating punch in the gut to the vice president of the Pre-Bar Association of the New York University School of Law. Calmly, he said, "That's okay, I'll stay with my aunt. She lives in D.C." I was not as gracious. In anger, I barked, "You don't accept my friend, you don't get us, you creep." And borrowing from some of the army's vernacular, I added, "And you can take this bigoted hotel and shove it up your ass."

With that off my chest, the three of us stormed out of the lobby despite the entreaties of my friend that my wife and I check in, and that he would be just fine. "No way," I told him. I was outraged that the conference planners had chosen such a bigoted venue, and in our nation's capital no less. We all returned to my car and headed back to New York. The shock to my wife and me was that such bigotry existed in D.C. despite a war in which so many African Americans fought and died for their country that treated them so shamefully.

The NYU law school board was equally shocked when I reported the disgraceful incident to them. The irony is that my friend, the vice president of the Pre-Bar Association, the young man who was denied admission to the hotel because he was a "Negro", became the first black judge of New York's Court of Appeals, the state's highest judicial body. Obviously, that outrageous and sickening experience was not one of the greatest days of my life.

A SINGER NAMED "JOHNNY LOMBARDO"

Passing the bar and starting a law practice was no easy task. Having married Pearl in 1948 (during the first semester of law school), I joined Local 802 of the musician's union and played club dates at weddings, Bar Mitzvahs, and other events as a sax man and singer just to keep up with my bills.

At one of the music gigs, a guest came up to me. He introduced himself as the owner of WHOM, a New York radio station that catered mostly to an Italian audience. He invited me to participate in one of his Sunday morning shows—a singing contest. The radio program was a one-hour competition in which the winner was chosen from call-ins combined with the votes of two judges in the radio studio who would then select and announce the winner (almost a precursor to the popular TV success, "American Idol"). The winning first prize was a professional photoshoot with Oggiano, a renowned theatrical celebrity photographer.

I accepted his invitation to compete on the show but thought I would have a better shot if I used a name that sounded Italian. So, for that contest, I changed my name to "Johnny Lombardo". As for the song selection, a most popular music name at the time was Arthur Tracey, who carried the moniker of, "The Street Singer". His very popular signature number was, "Marta, Rambling Rose of the Wildwood", a song he would always sing to open up his own nationally syndicated radio show.

Since the WHOM singing contest featured its own small string orchestra (piano, violin, viola, cello, and string bass), I orchestrated a special arrangement for the five instruments. I distributed the sheet music to the ensemble a few minutes before the live broadcast, and went through a quick rehearsal.

I knew I needed a handle to distinguish me from the other very talented contestants. Some sang arias from Italian operas, others sang Italian love songs, and so on. If I had any chance at all, I had to be different—and I was. After the orchestral introduction I had composed, I sang one chorus of "Marta" in English. Following an eight-bar musical segue, and to everyone's surprise, I picked up my alto sax and played a full chorus of "Marta". I then returned to the last thirty-two bars, sixteen of which were sung with a full-throated ending in Italian. I had received a translation from a neighbor and rehearsed the Italian pronunciation of the words many times to make sure they sounded authentic enough to pass muster.

Amazingly, "Johnny Lombardo" won first prize. This was my ticket to Oggiano's celebrity studio where he took a number of photographs under special lighting, some of which I have to this day, 65 years later. The back of one of the photos is inscribed, "To Johnny Lombardo, the winner," and signed by the owner of WHOM and Oggiano.

But despite the thrill of winning, it still was not the greatest day of my life.

MY PERSONAL MANAGER
AND ENTERTAINMENT CAREER

Sometime after the "Johnny Lombardo" incident, while playing sax and singing with my band at a wedding in a large Brooklyn hall on Eastern Parkway (I would average four to five club dates a week), a man in his 30's approached me after I had performed one of my signature routines—an Al Jolson medley. He introduced himself as "Lee Magid", telling me he was the personal manager of Della Reese, the popular black singer. He  added that he was the "A and R" man of a well-known record company. I knew that "A and R" was industry jargon for "Artists and Repertoire" and that one with that title was an extremely important executive in the record business. In fact, at the time, he was in charge of selecting artists and songs for Savoy and Regent Records over which he had exclusive control. "How would you like to make four sides on the Regent label?" he asked with a telling wink. I was shocked and responded with dead silence. "The deal is, I also become your personal manager." Wow.

Within a week, I was at a professional recording studio located at 1650 Broadway, cutting four sides. The songs I had suggested which were approved by Lee, were in the Jolson genre and picked out of the library of the famous song publishers, Shapiro and Bernstein. The handle this time was that I change my show biz name to Lennie "Mr. Dixie" Forrest, and that I record the songs with a bluegrass background sound, banjo and all. In addition, when performing on stage, that I wear polka-dot gloves and a Kentucky style polka-dot bow tie. That garb as my look, we thought, would be unique shtick and a stick-out from the other boy singers.

My first record, "Mammy of Mine", was released, backed by, "Dixie Train"— on 78's of course. In that era, while *Variety Magazine* traditionally featured Hollywood actors, two widely distributed national trade mags featured new recording artists. They were *Billboard* and *Cashbox*. Each magazine showcased the new record releases of the week which was a huge promotion for the Jukebox industry. The mags also featured the, "Record Sleeper of the Week", a most important indicator of what would hit the future charts. One of the critic picks was a young talented singer who had performed on the very popular Arthur Godfrey network TV talent show. His winning song which also became his first record release on the King label was, "Poinciana". The singer—Steve Lawrence. Another critic pick was Lennie "Mr. Dixie" Forrest and my breakout recording of, "Mammy of Mine". Each of us was lauded by *Billboard* and *Cashbox* as the "Boy singing stars of the future." Entertainment columns in the local press made similar predictions.

MY SIGNING A CONTRACT WITH
MUSIC CORPORATION OF AMERICA (MCA)

The kudos didn't escape the watchful eyes of MCA (Music Corporation of America), the then largest theatrical agency in the world. The hot call came from Lee Magid, my personal manager. He excitedly reported that Bobby Brenner, a top MCA agent had offered me a contract. It was fantastic news and a possible opening to a big show biz career.

Through MCA, I was booked into upscale supper clubs, nightclubs, and large entertainment venues throughout the country. In addition to TV and radio, I was even featured with the late Tommy Dorsey orchestra under the then baton of Buddy "Night-Train" Morrow in a mammoth Dallas, Ft. Worth entertainment palace called, "Pappy's Showland".

My wife Pearl was my traveling companion and biggest booster. Often, I would cross paths with Steve Lawrence, who too had been signed up by MCA. He would either be entering or exiting a radio station in Philly, Chicago, Boston, or some other big record market where we would meet with DJ's, trying to induce them to promote our records. Steve lucked out and hooked up with *The Steve Allen Show*, the precursor to the Johnny Carson *Tonight Show*. It was there that he met the magnificently talented Eydie Gorme, married her, and performed all over the world as, "Steve and Eydie".

Eydie Gorme whose real last name was "Gormanzano", of Sephardic Jewish heritage, coincidently was a distant relative of mine. In fact, she even did a gig with my band when I was booked to play a large college dance. It was prior to her great fame in the music business, but even then, with a magical singing voice and style, I knew Eydie was on her way to a giant show biz career.

MY MEET WITH THE
MASTER ENTERTAINER AL JOLSON

In early 1950, while in my last year of law school, I was working in a non-descript New York night club when between shows I would usually return to a small dingy dressing room and try to catch up with some of my classwork.

There was a knock on the door. "Who's there?" I called out. "Someone's here to see you." "Come on in," I responded, wondering who that could be. *"Being pretty current with my bills, it couldn't be a process server,"* I hoped.

The door opened and when I saw who it was, I was blown away. It was "Jolie", himself. Al Jolson. My knees felt wobbly, like I would keel over. "Mr. Jolson," were the only words that my surprised brain could come up with. "Jolie" picked up the next line. "A friend of mine told me you do a terrific job. I heard a little bit tonight and I think he was right. Keep it up and you'll do okay, kid."

All I could muster up was, "I'm so honored. Thank you, Mr. Jolson." We shook hands and he left. It all happened in less than three minutes but the memory of that brief encounter, with the master entertainer himself, has remained with me as one of the very special moments of my life for more than 66 years.

MY HOLLYWOOD AUDITION FOR "THE JAZZ SINGER"

I too came close to some form of stardom in 1952 when called by MCA to audition for the movie lead in the Hollywood remake of the Jolson classic, "The Jazz Singer". For the audition, I sang my traditional Jolson medley. Seeing the approving smiles on the faces of the studio people present made me feel optimistic about getting the role. But although I received high marks from the producers and director, the head money-man of the film insisted upon a big name. Danny Thomas got the call. My personal manager Lee Magid and my MCA agent Bobby Brenner who attended, said that with my voice, personality, and versatility to be able to sing a cantorial piece, "Kol Nidre", (the Jewish prayer sung in the movie), I should have gotten the part. But that's history.

As a consolation prize, I was booked to open the Al Jolson Memorial Show before 18,000 people at New York's Madison Square Garden. In addition to my being booked with other celebrities in the line-up, I was also asked to sing the national anthem. I had sung it hundreds of times at a zllion affairs and never screwed up the words, something every singer will admit to having done at some time. Now the story... After the orchestral introduction, I completely blanked out on the first line of the lyrics. Do that and you're dead meat for the balance of the anthem. What was Francis Scott Key smoking when he used all those words? So this is what I did... I performed our country's national anthem with words I was making up and rhyming as I kept on singing. Surprisingly, when I finished with what I thought was a disaster, people came up to me and said how much they enjoyed the second stanza which they had never heard before. True story.

Fortunately, when it came my turn to perform, I felt far more secure singing my signature Jolson medley opening up with, "Swanee", followed by "April Showers", "Toot Toot Tootsie", "Anniversary Song", and ending up on my knees with a big finish of "Mammy". The exposure landed me a steady singing spot on the New York daily ABC-TV Joe Franklin "Memory Lane" show.

And although it was real cool being in front of the TV cameras, it was still not the greatest day of my life.

MY "BORSCHT BELT" EXPERIENCES

I cannot look back upon my life without mentioning my singing career in the "Borscht Belt". "Borscht Belt"? Ah yes, that Jewish paradise in the heart of the Catskill Mountains just 90 miles from New York City. Take the George Washington Bridge to New Jersey. Get onto Route 17 and you'd be heading Northwest to such towns as Fallsburg, Loch Sheldrake, Monticello, Liberty, and the home of hundreds of hotels that provided fresh bagels and lox combined with clean mountain air. It was a very special area that catered to vacationing Jews who mostly came from

Brooklyn and the Bronx in the 1930's, 40's, and 50's. Three full meals, hourly sports, lawn exercises, games like "Simon Says", social activities, and nightly entertainment in what was called "the casino", was standard fare.

Many of the show biz biggies launched their careers in the "Borscht Belt", also known as the "Jewish Alps": Sid Caesar, Jerry Lewis, Milton Berle, Eddie Fischer, Red Buttons, and a long list of entertainment stars. Although not in their league, I began working in "the mountains" (another name for "Borscht Belt") as a musician in bands even before WWII. In addition to other amenities, the "Belt" was a natural gathering place for young people who met, fell in love and later married, which takes me to one of the greatest moments of my life...

It was the summer of 1946, the war was over and I was sent home from the Philippines to be discharged from the army. Having been in the Pacific theater and away from home for many months, upon my return stateside, I was given a short furlough prior to my final discharge. Pending my exit from the army, I had the option to wear civvies or my uniform, and thus purchased some civilian outfits. After being at home for several days, I took my mother to the Brickman Hotel in South Fallsburg, having packed my new civilian clothes and my army uniform.

MY MEETING PEARL AND A NIGHT TO REMEMBER

We arrived at the hotel and checked in just before dinner. After freshening up, we went to the dining room and were escorted to a table set for ten guests. Eight were already seated and we sat in the remaining two seats. To my right was a moderately attractive girl. She (who I will call, "Dorothy") and I decided to walk to the casino. In those days, the "casino" was the large ballroom where the band played, people danced, and gathered socially.

Unlike today's "casino", it was not a place for gambling. The hotel guests would usually gather there after dinner. When we arrived at the entrance door, I spotted a young girl dressed in a black shirt with matching tight pants. To my eyes, she was the most beautiful girl I had ever seen. I said to myself, "That's the one I really want to be with tonight." But she was with a young man (who I will call, "Bill"). I immediately went over to this perfect stranger, stuck out my right hand and said, "Hi, my name is Lenny. What's yours?" He said his name was "Bill." Without skipping a beat, I said, "Bill, I'd like you to meet Dorothy." Even before the social exchanges, I elbowed my way quickly and asked, "And what's your name?" Taken by surprise, she answered, "Pearl." Within an instant, and with much bravado, I took Pearl by the arm and whisked her away, leaving Dorothy and Bill open-mouthed and bewildered. But who cared? I accomplished what I set out to do. With a fast pace, and Pearl wondering what had just happened, I walked her to my new 1946 Chevy my father had given me as a "coming home from the war" present, started it up, and took off fast.

I drove to Monticello, a few miles up the road, conversing with Pearl all the way. Not only was she beautiful, but she also had such a sweet manner about her. We drove to a soda shop, took a table in a corner, and ordered two soft drinks. We sat and talked, totally oblivious of who, or what, was around us. The chemistry was all there.

On our drive back to the hotel, I leaned over to the right and attempted to kiss her. The road was dark and curvy and I almost drove into a ditch. Startled, but regaining control, we both shared a good laugh.

When we arrived back at the Brickman Hotel, we spoke again for more than an hour. I knew then that Pearl would become a part of my life. It was, as it is often said, "love at first sight," and I could feel it all happening. Before we said goodnight (and this time I did kiss her without driving into a hazard), we made a date to be seated at the same table in the dining room and that I would make the necessary arrangements with the maître d'.

Although I was wearing civvies when we first met, I decided to dress up in my army uniform for dinner. I had told Pearl the night before that I was still in the service, to be officially discharged in a month, but I deliberately did not tell her my rank. The uniform, in fact, was my dress uniform as a first lieutenant in the army field artillery with all of the ribbons I had received for my military service, which included my oversees duty in the Pacific.

Seeing me in my army officer's uniform must have sealed the deal since we went steady almost immediately, became engaged one year later, and married at the Park Central Hotel in Manhattan on December 26, 1948.

Although I had gone out with many girls before I ever met Pearl, she was the only one I ever fell in love with—a love that lasted almost sixty-eight years of a wonderful marriage.

MY BEING BOOKED AS SOCIAL DIRECTOR

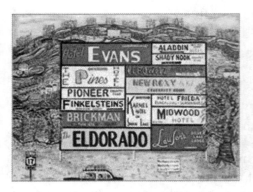

Looking back upon those glorious days, the "Borscht Belt" was a haven of excitement, fun, and romance, where hundreds of other couples traced their first real romantic encounter at one of the area's hotels, as did I.

As for the many summers post World War II, I would be booked at different resort hotels, receive room and board for my wife and I in addition to $100 or so a week. For those days, it was considered a pretty good deal.

As the social director, it was my job to arrange all of the guest activities, and perform as the MC each night in the casino. When it was "show time", I would open it up with a spirited song or two, and then introduce the star attraction who would usually be a well-known comic such as Buddy Hackett, Joan Rivers, Henny Youngman, Dick Shawn, Red Buttons, Jack Carter, or some other marquis name. I would also be booked at other popular area hotels as the Concord, Grossinger's, Brown's, Kutsher's, Pioneer, and many more. Charlie Rapp, Hal Edwards, and Mort Curtis, three of the area's biggest theatrical agents, kept me busy with club date bookings throughout the summer season.

But even with all my enjoyable entertainment experiences, none rose to being the greatest day of my life.

TAKE YOUR PARTNER TO THE LEFT AND DO-SI-DO

I had heard good things about The Ambassador Hotel, one in which I was never booked. It was located in South Fallsburg, right in the heart of the "Belt", and I had to find some way to make a connection. That said, there is a back-story that deserves a mention. It goes something like this... I was booked

as the social director at the Naponach Hotel near Ellenville, NY during the summer of 1949. While it was a nice resort, I was searching out some angle that would give me an introduction to the Ambassador's owner.

Call it serendipity, but a professional square dance caller stayed at the Naponach Hotel and used it as his home base for the summer and would book all of his club dates to other hotels from there. My wife Pearl, he, and I would usually sit at the same table for lunch at the Naponach Hotel. During lunch one afternoon, he complained that he wasn't feeling well and that he was looking for a substitute square dance caller for the hotel in which he had been booked. By coincidence, the hotel in question was The Ambassador. Without hesitation, I told him to look no further since I would sub for him. Despite my never having called a square dance in my life, I assured him that I had conducted many square dances and knew the drill. Hearing that, he telephoned the Ambassador's owner, told him he was ill, but that he had arranged for a substitute caller. Although disappointed, and there not being sufficient time to arrange for another program, the owner reluctantly agreed.

Getting the go sign, Pearl and I immediately drove to the public library in Ellenville, searched out the books on square dancing, and borrowed the only one we could find. We then looked for a general store. Drove around the town and found one. There, we bought two straw cowboy hats, checkered shirts, denims, and red bandanas. After all, if I was to call a square dance, I had to at least look the part. And Pearl had to be outfitted as a cowgirl as well.

We returned to the hotel as fast as we could. Time was running out and I still had to read the book taken out of the library to learn about square dancing and how to call it. I had to find at least one that I could call without making an ass of myself. Talk about pressure and risk-taking, I finally selected, "Pop Goes the Weasel", since it looked simple enough for me to bluff my way through a call. There was no time left for me to try to find another dance. We still had to have some dinner, get dressed, and had a thirty-minute drive ahead of us. And the clock was not my ally.

AT THE AMBASSADOR HOTEL

 We arrived at The Ambassador a little after 8 pm in our Western get-up. My anxiety level rose even more when I saw that my name had already been posted on the entertainment board in the lobby of the hotel as the square dance caller for the evening's program. By 8:45, the guests were already filing out of the dining room and heading toward the casino for an evening of square dancing.

Having been in the music business for some time, I knew most of the musicians in the band who were setting up on the casino stage. I also knew the leader, Buddy White, having worked together as members of Local 802 of the musicians' union. When he saw me in my cowboy digs, and hearing that I was subbing for the caller, his surprised comment was, "What the hell are you doing here, Lenny? You're no square dance guy." Nervously, I responded, "Buddy, that's our little secret. Be a pal and just follow what I ask and I hope everything turns out okay."

By 9 pm the guests were gathered in the casino. Many were dressed in Western outfits in keeping with the evening's program. A few minutes later, while trying to hold back his laughter, Buddy took the microphone and introduced me as the evening's square dance caller. He then passed the hand mic to me with a quizzical look that said, "You're on your own. Now what, pal?" With the mic in hand, I told the guests gathered there in the center of the floor that we were going to have a great evening together. With that, I gave the cue to Buddy to play the introduction to, "Pop Goes the Weasel".

From the corner of my eye I could see Pearl sitting next to the stage. She looked even more nervous than I was. The music started and with a false bravado, I called the dance while Buddy's band played loudly behind me. After about ten minutes of, "Take your partner to the left, swing her around, and do-si-do," and so on, I finished, "Pop Goes the Weasel", the only square dance I learned from the library book I borrowed. When the dance was over, there was a smattering of mild applause as the guests looked in my direction waiting for the next dance to be called. What do I do now?

Buddy looked at me with a curious eye and a shrug. I also caught a glimpse of Pearl who appeared extremely anxious. I spotted Mr. Hymie Merle, the owner of The Ambassador staring at me. He had booked many square dance callers throughout the years of his hotel ownership, and what he just witnessed raised his eyebrows with deep suspicion.

Well, this was my big moment, but also a big risk. Do I blow it or do I make it happen? "Okay folks," I rang out, removing my cowboy hat, the inside brim of which was wet with sweat, "this is what I want you to do. Each of you take one of the chairs from the side of the wall" (they had been stacked there for the square dance). "Carry a chair and set it down show-style in front of the stage." Looking toward Buddy, I said, "Play some setting-up chair music." No one had a clue what was happening, including Mr. Merle who was as much in the dark as everyone else.

NOT EXACTLY A SQUARE DANCE

When all were seated, and facing me, I whispered in Buddy's ear, gave him the music key and the title of a popular song. I also asked that the overhead house lights be turned off. "Folks, sit back and relax. Maestro White, introduction please." For the next hour, I put on a singing and comedy show for the audience. Guests who were outside and not too wild about square dancing, suddenly started to slowly file into the casino. Each picked up a chair and quickly became part of the listening audience.

I gave the guests my full club-date routine including popular standards, songs in Italian, French, my Jolson medley, Jewish and cantorial favorites, with some comedy banter mixed in. When I finished my act (after several encores), the audience gave me a standing ovation, wild cheers, whistles, and prolonged applause. I didn't deliver a square dance, but they received an evening of entertainment they never expected. Their enthusiasm and response made me feel like a rock star, all of which caught the very surprised and approving attention of Mr. Merle, Ambassador's owner.

When it was over, he came to me, and speaking with a heavy Jewish accent, said, "I know you're not a square dance caller Lenny, but you're a terrific entertainer. So tell me, where you working?" I told him, "The Naponach Hotel." Right then and there, he offered me the job as MC and social director for the next summer season. The terms we agreed upon were right. I accepted the deal and he asked that I follow him to his office. I then drew up a one-page letter agreement sealing the bargain.

The night could have been a disaster, but fortunately, it turned out the other way. And with all the compliments from the guests, in addition to getting the summer job I had been seeking, it was a really big win.

But despite the accolades, it still did not add up to the greatest day of my life.

MY ROLE AS MC AT
THE MOULIN ROUGE NIGHT CLUB

I worked at the Ambassador the next summer season, the summer after that, and was booked as the MC for a third summer season.

It was the summer of 1952, when the first nightclub-style facility was added to the hotel. It was a glitzy addition called the Moulin Rouge Club of the Ambassador. It had all the earmarks of an upscale supper club. As a comparison, I had been to the famous Copacabana in Manhattan many times (my HSMA classmate, Al Foster, was the music director at the Copa), and found that the Moulin Rouge Club was fancier, more attractive, with far more guest comforts. It had a most striking appearance even more so than The Latin Quarter, another popular night club in Manhattan, which was owned and operated by Lou Walters, the father of Barbara Walters. The stage had brilliant gold painted columns on each side, with walls that were faux painted in burgundy and gold striping. The center of the club was adorned with round tables supported by carved wooden legs. The tabletops were covered by shining burgundy fabric with matching burgundy and gold chairs. Colorful paintings on the perimeter walls depicted French scenes with a strikingly beautiful large scene of the Eifel Tower on the wall of the club's entrance. The big eye-catcher was the huge chandelier that hung in the center of the club with its many tiers of lights and brilliant sparkles. The Moulin Rouge was indeed a jewel, and the envy of other hotel owners in the "Borscht Circuit".

The Moulin Rouge also served as an upscale venue and showcase for me that summer, but still, no evening, despite all the razzmatazz, measured up to being the greatest day of my life.

I'M WATCHING THE ED SULLIVAN SHOW

In the early days of television, certain special shows were so dominant that the nights they were televised were even named after them; the "I Love Lucy" night; the "Sid Caesar" night; the "Milton Berle" night; the "Mash" night, and so on. And of course, Sunday was always the "Ed Sullivan" night.

During one of the Sullivan shows, he announced that his guest the following Sunday would be the Reverend Billy Graham. He also stated that on the Friday before the Sunday Sullivan show, Graham would be holding a major Evangelical rally at Madison Square Garden with a full house of twenty thousand followers expected to attend. This was "really big" (using the Sullivan signature phrase). Upon hearing that announcement, a light bulb went off. In addition to my other avocations, I was also a song-writer. A few weeks prior to the Sullivan blurb, I had composed the music and lyrics to an inspirational song titled, "The Man". Immediately, I related the character to the Reverend Billy Graham, although when I composed it, he was nowhere in my thoughts. An idea suddenly struck me. If I could produce a record with me singing, "The Man", and if it could be personally presented to Reverend Billy Graham crediting him as the song's inspiration, it would be a major PR coup that could give me a giant show biz boost. These are the lyrics and judge for yourself...

"THE MAN"

His eyes were clear
His voice was warm
His face a golden tan
He gave no name
Nor whence he came
I knew him as just "The Man"

He looked at me
We spoke our minds
As sometimes strangers can
My heart was low
I felt it glow
The day that I met "The Man"

I saw he was kind and worldly
With wisdom that few attain
I cried out to him please help me
Oh why is there so much pain

He answered me
There's misery in life without a plan
Take heart don't grieve
And just believe

He spoke and my life began
I'll never forget "The Man"

*The Graham story is continued on page 62...

I am on a club date when requested by radio station owner of WHOM to compete in a singing competition. Circa 1951.

This is a demo record of "Marta", the song I sang, and played on the alto sax for the competition held on radio station WHOM. Circa 1951.

I am singing at
one of my club dates.

50

One of the photos taken by Oggiano, the celebrity photographer, as the winning first prize where I performed as "Johnny Lombardo", in the radio station WHOM singing contest. Circa 1951.

One of the celebrity photos taken by Oggiono for winning first prize as "Johnny Lombardo" in the radio station WHOM singing contest. Circa 1951.

I am the social director at the Napanoch Hotel, NY.
Those guests who participated in all daily activities received diplomas, as shown. 1951.

I just completed a show calling upon the hotel guests on stage who participated
as part of the evening's entertainment. Each guest would thereafter
receive a complimentary bottle of champagne. I am kneeling, and in the circle. 1951.

The New York newspapers would normally carry pages of hotels advertising the Borscht Circuit. The above has a photo of me as director of activities at one of the hotels. 1951.

I am seated third from the left next to Pearl.
Others are guests in the hotel where I was the social director. 1951.

The Hotel Brickman, in the Borscht Belt is where I met Pearl. We became engaged in 1947, and married in 1948, a marriage that lasted almost 68 years. 1946.

A guest photo was taken at the end of the week at The Brickman Hotel. Pearl and I (encircled), Pearl's mother is to the left (encircled), and my mother (encircled) is to the right. 1946.

1946 photo taken with Pearl the second night we met. On the first night, since I was soon to
be discharged from the army, I was authorized to wear civilian clothes.
The next night, I surprised her by wearing my army officer's dress uniform.
I had just returned from the Philippines and was scheduled for discharge in one month.
The chemistry was all there and it was indeed, "Love at first sight."
We were engaged one year later, and married one year after that, in 1948.

My late beautiful wife Pearl. 1946.

My late wonderful wife at a hotel
in the "Borscht Belt." 1946.

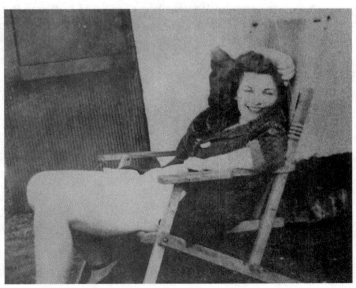

My first car given to me as a, "Home from the war", gift from my father.
New cars at that time could only be sold to or for veterans.
This was a beautiful 1946 maroon Chevy. The Brickman Hotel is in the background.
The car is the one I drove to whisk Pearl away the first night we met. 1946.

Guests in the indoor pool of the hotel. 1954.

Guests on the golf course of the hotel. 1954.

I was the MC at the Moulin Rouge, the new addition to the Ambassador Hotel,
In South Fallsburg, NY. It was a plush upscale night club where I worked with
some of the biggest names in show business. 1954.

The flyer sent by my personal manager to theatrical agents. 1954.

MY CALL TO BILLY GRAHAM THE FIGHTER

 I had only five days to put the moving parts together. But even more importantly, I needed a sure-fire handle. And I found one. To begin with, Billy Graham, the Reverend, was a household name. I came up with another household name, Billy Graham, the professional boxer who almost became the middleweight champion of the world. But where would I find Billy Graham, the fighter, now? And even if I could locate him, how could I make him a part of what I was hoping to do? This was my plan laid out in many steps...

Step one... the Monday morning following the Sullivan show, I telephoned the sports editor of the Long Island Press, a major Newhouse newspaper at the time. If anyone would know where Graham the fighter could be found, it would be he—and I was right. The sports editor told me that Graham was now employed as a good-will ambassador for a popular brewery in Brooklyn. I telephoned the number given to me, asked to speak to Billy, and was told he was in the field, but that he generally called in every two hours. I gave my name, phone number, and the name of the Long Island Press's sports editor. I told the receptionist that it was urgent he call me without delay. One hour later, I received a phone call from Graham and told him it was important that we meet. Unbeknown to me, he had already called the sports editor who confirmed that I was legitimate, and since by happenstance he was in Queens, we arranged to meet at a local diner.

The last time I had seen Billy Graham, he was in boxing shorts going twelve rounds with Kid Gavilan in a bruising fight for the welterweight championship title of the world. When he appeared at the diner however, he was decked out in a navy blue tailored suit, white shirt and red-striped tie. Although his nose was spread out a bit from the many times it was pounded and broken in the ring, he had the look of a successful executive.

I introduced myself and shared my idea. Telling him that I had composed a song, "The Man." I added that I would record it with a full orchestra on Thursday, and that a record would be presented to the Reverend Billy Graham on Friday. That the presentation of "The Man" would be made at a fully-covered press conference to be held at Madison Square Garden two hours prior to the Reverend's giant rally. Of course, this was all wishful talk. He asked where he fit in and what his involvement would be. I told him he could substitute a few words of the lyrics and that as a result, he would become a co-writer of "The Man".

The PR angle, I stressed, was that he would present the record to the Reverend Billy Graham, who in turn would acknowledge Billy Graham the fighter, as a great God-loving Born Again Christian. I told him that once again he would be at the Garden, not where he fought many times, but in a completely different role, and with a namesake that was admired by millions throughout the world. As an added incentive, I offered him twenty percent of all royalties from the sale of the record. It was a win-win deal, I urged.

Graham agreed. He changed a few words of the lyrics, and I drew up a one- paragraph agreement. Step one was now complete, and all of it accomplished only one day following the Sullivan show.

MY CALL TO JOHNNIE RAY

Step two... Having Billy Graham, the fighter, on board, I called Lee Magid, my personal manager, and asked him to get word to Johnnie Ray, a top recording artist who had been introduced to me by Lee and to set up a phone call for me. Lee came through and I phoned Johnnie Ray, who had a blockbuster record hit with "Cry". I finally reached Johnnie in the late afternoon and asked him to call Perry Alexander, the publisher of "Cry",  to request that he see me the next day on a matter of great importance. Johnnie Ray came through mostly as a favor to Lee Magid.

MY MEET WITH PUBLISHER PERRY ALEXANDER

On Tuesday, the next morning, I went to 1619 Broadway, known as, "The Brill Building", and was escorted into Perry's office. I brought a piano player with me knowing I would have to sing "The Man" to Alexander if there was any chance that he would agree to publish it. I told him the unique handle was that Billy Graham, the fighter, was also a co-writer of the song, and that he would personally present a special recording of it to Billy Graham, the Reverend, at a press conference to be held at Madison Square Garden on Friday. Immediately, I sensed his interest when he asked me to sing "The Man" for him. I sang one chorus after which he said it was an okay song. He would ordinarily say something like, "I'll call you if I'm interested." But with the "Graham meets Graham" twist, combined with all the other hype I was feeding him, most of which was hopeful fantasy, surprisingly, he agreed to publish it. His consent took care of step two.

MY CALL TO BILLY GRAHAM THE REVEREND

Step three... I now had to reach out to Reverend Billy Graham. If I could not locate him, or if he refused to go along with the record idea, the whole plan would have been a total zero. After a dozen telephone calls, I finally reached the Reverend's PR person and laid out all of my ideas. I told him that Billy Graham, the middle weight champ, had written a song that described the great character of Billy Graham the Reverend. That it was published by Perry Alexander, the famous publisher of the mega hit, "Cry". That Billy Graham, the fighter, hoped he could be converted into becoming a Born Again Christian. That he, Billy Graham, the fighter, would present the recording of "The Man" to Billy Graham, the Reverend. That a press conference with tons of media would be held at Madison Square Garden two hours before the big rally. With plenty of "sell", the clincher was that twenty-five percent of the proceeds from all record sales of "The Man" would go directly to the Reverend Billy Graham Foundation. After digesting the upside of the pitch, he finally gave his approval. Step three, a real chancy one, was now covered like a blanket.

MY CALL TO ORCHESTRA LEADER
AND ARRANGER NAT BROOKS

Step four... It was late Tuesday afternoon, only two days after the Sullivan show, when I telephoned Nat Brooks, a popular orchestra leader and music arranger. He was a friend and one with whom I had played many club dates. I filled him in with the whole "Billy Graham" handle, that Perry Alexander was the publisher of "The Man", and that both Graham the fighter and Graham the Reverend were fully on board. I also related that a press conference would be held at Madison Square Garden just three days away with all the media in attendance, and that time was of the essence. After giving him all the information I had up to that moment, I told him I had to have an arrangement of "The Man" immediately, in addition to his orchestra for the recording session I had already booked at the Nola studios set for Thursday morning. Brooks fell in love with the whole concept and the high-stakes PR promotion of the record, but he had to make certain that what I pitched to him was not fabricated. After making a number of phone calls to the players involved, he was satisfied that I was leveling with him. He did have one condition however, that one of the songs he had composed, "The Eighth Wonder of the World", would have to be on the flip side of "The Man". Of course, I agreed. With that, an excited Nat Brooks said he would even add a choral background to his orchestra. Step four was now behind me.

Step five... Nat Brooks spent Wednesday orchestrating "The Man" having received the sheet music from the publisher Perry Alexander the day before.

MY RECORDING OF "THE MAN" AT NOLA STUDIOS

It was now Thursday morning at the Nola studios. I had booked two hours which would provide plenty of time for a rehearsal and as many takes as needed. Nat Brooks was in the studio with a ten-piece orchestra and four background singers. We rehearsed "The Man", and "Eighth Wonder of the World", with orchestra and choral background. Considering the short time Brooks had to orchestrate "The Man", he had done a masterful job. No wonder he was considered one of the best in the business! After the rehearsals, the two sides were cut, and after only three takes. A studio engineer in the sealed control room balanced the sound and was already working on the masters. The session worked out to perfection and the recordings sounded first-rate.

On Wednesday, the day before, I had already ordered five hundred records from a commercial manufacturer to be pressed from the master recording. The printing of labels and cover envelopes for a 45-rpm record were also ordered. On Thursday, I also had a press release hand delivered to all the New York media with the flash that Billy Graham the fighter would present Billy Graham the Reverend with a recording of "The Man", which he co-wrote, and that the conference would be held in the press room of Madison Square Garden on Friday, two hours before the big rally. That Graham the fighter was so inspired by Graham the Reverend that he would become a Born Again Christian. I followed up with phone calls and was amazed by the enthusiastic response. Step five had worked like magic.

BILLY GRAHAM MEETS BILLY GRAHAM

Step six... The press conference was a huge success. AP, UPI, radio, TV and print media were all there. Dozens of photos were taken, some which had me holding up the record of "The Man" with me in the middle of the two Grahams.

At the end of the conference, Billy and I were escorted to a VIP box to await the entrance of the Evangelical leader to the podium. Within ten minutes, Reverend Billy Graham appeared amidst the wild cheers and applause of the packed Garden. Following his opening prayers and greetings, he began his initial remarks by announcing that Billy Graham the fighter was present, and asked him to stand as bright spot beams were focused upon him. This created a mass eruption of applause by the thousands in attendance. I just sat there in wonderment as to how everything had come together so well. Indeed, step six was concluded without a flaw.

Step seven... Considering all the photos that were taken, together with the human-interest story of "Graham meets Graham", I had ordered a news clipping service. It provided me with the pictures and articles that appeared in hundreds of newspapers in cities throughout the country. In fact, since there was a fee attached to each clipping sent to me, there were so many, that I had to cancel the service. Step seven, although most successful, was getting far too expensive for me to continue with it.

Step eight... I sent the record of "The Man" to DJ's in three major cities: New York, Boston, and Chicago. The record was enclosed in a packet that contained news clippings and a personal letter from Billy Graham the fighter. While the record received fairly good plays, it didn't break through to the top-list charts of the industry. On the upside, however, I had done what most would have considered an impossible feat, and did it all from scratch in five days.

Although I felt a strong sense of accomplishment, the end result did not lead to one of the greatest days of my life. As an aside, I was told that the record was sold recently on E-Bay for $40.

67

At the beach on an afternoon with Pearl in Cape Cod, MA, where I was the featured singer in an upscale supper club in the evening.
1954.

This is the record that launched my entertainment career.
1952.

One of the ads featured
in Cashbox magazine.
1952.

13   May 31, 1952

IT'S NEW
IT'S DIFFERENT
BOTH SIDES A HIT

LENNIE
(MR. DIXIE)
FORREST

HE TOPS
'EM ALL!

Singing...

"MAMMY
OF MINE"
Published By SHAPIRO-BERNSTEIN
1270 Sixth Ave., New York, N.Y.

"DIXIE
TRAIN"
Published By T.V. MUSIC COMPANY
1650 Broadway, New York, N.Y.

LENNIE (Mr. Dixie) FORREST

My recording of "Dixie Train".
My publicity photo is at
the bottom of the record.
1952.

One of my signature
publicity photos with
polka dot gloves, and
a Kentucky style polka
dot tie. 1952.

Another publicity photo sent by
my personal manager and MCA
to theatrical agents throughout
the country. 1952.

On the beach in Cape Cod, MA, where I performed at night at a popular entertainment venue. 1954.

With Pearl on an afternoon at the beach in Cape Cod, MA, where I was the featured performer at an upscale supper club. 1954.

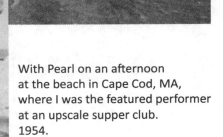

I am relaxing on the beach at Cape Cod, MA. Showtime was in a supper club in the evening. 1954.

My first record is released and picked by Cashbox magazine as the "Sleeper of the Week." I am in good company with singing stars, Steve Lawrence, Guy Mitchell and Frank Stevens. 1952.

My recording on Bell Records of "Rock-a-Bye Your Baby", having been inspired by the great entertainer, Al Jolson.

One of the promos circulated by my personal agent, and Music Corporation of America (MCA), to supper clubs throughout the country. 1954.

I am playing a Benny Goodman number on the clarinet with the band behind me. Circa 1950s.

Billy Graham the welterweight, meets Billy Graham the Reverend.
I'm on the right. All are holding my recording of, "The Man" at a press conference
held at Madison Square Garden, NYC, which I arranged.

My recording of, "The Man"
which was presented by
Billy Graham, the fighter, to
Billy Graham, the Reverend.

Here I am trying to keep in shape. Show biz had odd hours. Circa 1950's.

Here I am on a club date playing the tenor sax. Circa 1950's.

With Pearl, at a supper club in Dallas, Texas,
where I was the featured performer with The Tommy Dorsey Orchestra
under the direction of Buddy "Night Train" Morrow. Circa 1950's.

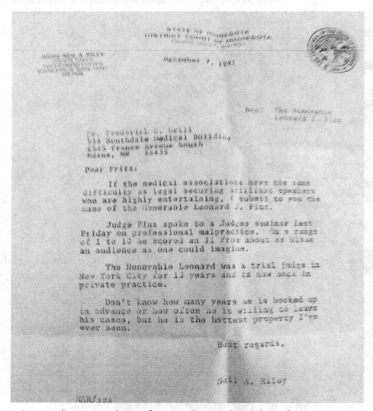

A complimentary letter from Judge Neil A. Riley of Minnesota.

The newspaper announcement of a dinner being held in my honor.

An advertisement featuring Lenny "Mr. Dixie" Forrest at Jimmy Fazio's, in Milwaukee, Wisconsin.

A critic's review of my performance at Jimmy Fazio's published in the Milwaukee Journal. 1952.

STARTING MY LAW CAREER

I set aside two years from law to try to make my breakthrough in the entertainment field. Although I came close to big things, almost making it didn't cut it. It was now time to finally devote my time to law. Lawyers usually remember the first case they ever handled, and I am no exception. I remember it all...

It started when I was sharing a pastrami sandwich at the famous Carnegie Deli, located in the heart of tin-pan-alley, with Lee Magid, my personal manager. As we got up to leave, Lee recognized a friend, Mort Curtis, sitting at one of the tables. We went over to him and Lee introduced me as one of his singers, and also a lawyer. Lee's friend was the owner of an advertising company, "The Curtis Adverting Agency". When Curtis heard I was a lawyer, his eyes lit up. He invited us to sit down, saying he wanted to discuss a legal matter with me. At the time, not only didn't I have a real office, but I didn't even have a single client. I did, however, have an office address at 150 Broadway in downtown Manhattan, with a phone number and a receptionist to take messages. To a client (if I would ever have one) it would appear as if it was my office being called, when in fact, it was nothing more than an answering service that I engaged (a common practice in those days) for $5 a month. Being able to use an address and telephone number, I had "Leonard L. Finz, Counselor at Law" cards printed as soon as I was admitted to the Bar.

MY ADVICE TO CURTIS

Back to Curtis...

He was angry that he had provided advertising to someone (who I will name Mr. Jones), and that he was owed $10,000. The ads he furnished referred to a seven-day exposition titled, "The International Winter Sports Show", being held at

Madison Square Garden. After hearing him out, I tried to sound lawyerly and told him I would contact Jones for him to see what if anything I could do to be of service. Apparently, Jones was an affluent man with a Park Avenue address, but like most business people, created a corporation specifically for the Madison Square Garden winter sports exposition in order to insulate himself from any personal liability.

The next morning, a Saturday, Curtis called me at home telling me that Jones needed $5,000 more of advertising, assuring Curtis that another ad promotion would "absolutely" boost lagging attendance at the Garden. In order to protect what was already owed, Curtis was edging toward extending additional credit to Jones. The reason for his call to me however, was to seek my advice as to how he could be protected if he honored the request and then later Jones defaulted in making payment.

Calling upon the Secured Transactions course I took as a student at NYU law school four years earlier, I told Curtis to write down what I was about to dictate to him, and have Jones sign it before providing the additional advertising. What I dictated was a statement to insure a personal undertaking by Jones. It covered the additional $5,000, but also included the $10,000 already owed. Further, that payment of the $15,000 owed would be made within an agreed date, and that Jones sign a personal confession of judgment. Finally, if Jones defaulted in any manner, the full judgment of $15,000 plus interest and costs would be entered and filed with the court, in addition to whatever other remedies the law provided. Curtis was impressed with what I had dictated and our call ended. I didn't know at the time that Jones had also stiffed electricians, carpenters, suppliers, models, clothiers, musicians, sign-painters, and other trades people he had engaged for the show. He also had not paid all of the rent due Madison Square Garden.

Curtis advanced the additional $5,000 for the cost of an ad after Jones signed the personal undertaking and confession of judgment I had dictated from the top of my head. Now, the bad news... Within several days, with continued falling attendance, "The International Winter Sports Show" shut down and filed for bankruptcy, leaving all the creditors to await the action of the bankruptcy court.

MY MEET WITH GOLIATH IN THE
BATTLEFIELD OF THE BANKRUPTCY COURT

In short order, Curtis received an official court notice that all creditors were to appear in ten days at the first hearing. Again, Curtis called me and asked that I represent his agency. I knew zippo about bankruptcy, not having taken such a course in law school. But I at least had ten days to read the federal statute and bone up on other procedural regulations on the subject.

On the morning scheduled for the bankruptcy hearing, I put on a grey suit (I would have preferred navy blue but didn't own one), white shirt, and dark tie. Pearl had gone to a leather goods store a few days before, bought me a briefcase and even had my initials put on it. When I left our apartment that morning, amidst kisses, good wishes and goodbyes, I really looked like a lawyer. I drove from our small apartment in Bayside, Queens to the United States courthouse at Foley Square, Manhattan. When I arrived, I was directed to the courtroom where the hearing was scheduled to be held. There, I met Mort Curtis, my first client. The seats were already filled with all the other trades people who were left out in the cold by Jones.

A few minutes later, a mix of five men of different ages, all of whom were carrying black attaché' brief cases, dressed in dark suits, white shirts, and conservative ties, looking like they just came out of a cookie cutter, entered the courtroom. They were senior and junior partners plus associates of Dewey, Ballantine, Bushby, Palmer, and Wood, the number one Wall Street law firm with about five hundred lawyers at the time. Real Goliaths. Their client? Madison Square Garden. And me? I was Leonard L. Finz, Esquire, all by myself, who had never had a single case, let alone a complicated bankruptcy one.

HERE COMES THE JUDGE

At 10 am, the court officer rang out, "All rise," etc. As the black robed judge took the bench, he said he would call upon the creditors to make a statement and that he would start with the ones owed the most and go down the list. The largest amount owed was to Madison Square Garden for unpaid rent, utility bills, security, etc. Curtis was the second highest creditor, while the trades people varied in amounts that were mostly under $1,000. He called for the Garden's counsel to make his statement. The Dewey, Ballantine entourage that looked more like cardboard mannequins, took seats at the counsel table. The senior partner rose and handed the judge a forty-five-page brief. Wall Street law firms always excelled at that, and their billing practices proved it. For the next forty minutes the Dewey lawyer passed documents to the judge that had been handed methodically over to him by his associates. The movement of documents was like an assembly line in the Chaplin movie, "Modern Times." To me, it looked comical, but then again, this was my first time in court and whatever natural nervousness I had was being tempered with bizarre amusement as to the mechanical actions of the stiff-necked crew. Now to the Dewey lawyer's argument...

For forty minutes, his overall theme was that the thousands of dollars of admission money collected at the box office windows and tied up in bankruptcy, was not part of the bankrupt estate to be shared with other creditors. He argued that the proceeds became the exclusive property of Madison Square Garden since the rental contract stated clearly that the Garden was a preferred creditor and thus had priority over any other creditors in the event of a default.

When he completed his arguments, the judge called out, "Curtis Advertising." It was now my turn. Remember, I had never appeared in court before, but I had appeared before hundreds of different types of audiences in my show biz career and had developed a sense of contact and delivery. This was no different, and I surely wasn't about to be intimidated by the dark-suited contingent, either.

MY ARGUMENT TO THE COURT
AND THE CREDITORS WHO HEARD IT

 Speaking in a rather booming voice, I, in essence, told the judge that any agreement entered into between the two principals involved could not affect the rights of my client who was not privy to their private contract. That the thousands of dollars being held belonged to all creditors, the Garden included, to be distributed on a percentage basis in accordance with the amounts owed. I spoke no more than fifteen minutes. None of the trades people chose to speak and the hearing was adjourned pending the election of a Trustee by the creditors.

After the judge left the bench, I was surrounded by many in the courtroom who retained me on a contingency basis. In essence, I was to receive an agreed percentage of any money I recovered for them. To sum it all up... I was later elected Trustee by the creditors, had many conferences with the court and Dewey lawyers, and ultimately settled the case on behalf of Curtis and the trades people. Each creditor, including Madison Square Garden, received approximately fifty cents on the dollar of what was owed, a good percentage for a bankruptcy case. The white-shoe Dewey Wall Street lawyers did not succeed, and the Goliaths found themselves quite humbled by a novice and a result they never expected.

As for Curtis, I brought a lawsuit in the Manhattan Supreme Court based upon Jones' personal undertaking I had dictated that Saturday morning. The trial was held within a month before a judge without a jury. Curtis was awarded a judgment in full, less what already had been received in the bankruptcy proceeding. With a great deal of time and effort on my part, the amount due was finally paid by Jones (subpoenas, contempt proceedings, depositions to locate assets, and every roadblock to avoid or delay payment was employed by Jones). I learned the hard way what law school never taught me: how a lawyer must deal effectively with the real world out there.

Despite my victory, it still was not the greatest day of my life.

EXPANDING MY LAW PRACTICE

Having a few clients, I now needed a real office and rented a small room in a suite of offices at 154 Nassau Street in Manhattan for twenty-five dollars a month. The office was so small that when you opened the door, it would hit the desk. But at the least it was a place with my own phone and typewriter where I could get out some work on the few cases I had. I still had to play club dates since the income from my practice was insufficient to provide for my family while trying to pay my bills on time. All of that started to change, however, when word got out to some of the Local 802 members of the American Federation of Musicians union, that one of their own was also a lawyer. Suddenly, I started to get calls from the many musicians I had worked with through the years, cases that mostly involved personal injury claims resulting from auto accidents in which they were involved. The quick settlements I made with insurance companies gave me the reputation with my fellow musicians that, "If you're involved in an accident, call Lenny Finz."

A MAKE-SHIFT STAGE AND A BIG SPLASH

Here's an example of how musicians sought me out. It's a sad story but also quite comical in a perverted way...

An affluent owner of an auto parts manufacturing plant, who had a huge estate in Maryland, hosted an elaborate party for more than one hundred special guests. It was to take place around his decorative Olympic sized pool. He engaged the finest caterer and booked Bill Harrington, one of the top high-society orchestra leaders in Manhattan, to play at poolside. Harrington also had his own popular radio show on New York's station, WNEW. While there were many high-quality bands in his city that he could have engaged, he would settle for nothing but the best and was prepared to pay handsomely. And hiring a big-name Manhattan society orchestra headed by the famed Bill Harrington, is what he wanted to further impress his guests.

In order to feature the orchestra, the host had an elaborate elevated stage erected with ascending levels situated at the edge of the pool where Harrington's twelve-piece orchestra would be positioned and perform.

All was going beautifully well for the first hour or so with guests on the lavish poolside, decked out in formal attire under the stars having cocktails and sumptuous delicacies as the orchestra played the popular songs featured in the latest Broadway musicals.

Suddenly, there was a crackling noise coming from the elevated stage. Within seconds, the newly constructed stage collapsed. Nine of the twelve musicians were tossed into the pool, instruments and all. (The collapse is the sad part. Seeing them splash with their instruments is the perverted, comical aspect to it.) Fortunately, there were only minor injuries, but their musical instruments (saxes, clarinets, drums, trombones, string bass, trumpets) were of the finest quality that only musicians in their special high society league would own and play. A fine instrument drowned in a pool of water could be seriously or irreparably damaged. In addition, their own tuxedos, shirts, and accessories were similarly damaged.

A few days after the accident, I received the calls. Within the week, I was retained by all of the musicians who suffered instrument damage. Some of them were worth thousands. I also represented those who sustained minor lacerations. Within two months of my being retained (record time), I entered negotiations with the insurance company that covered the host party giver and settled every case. As a result, word got around very quickly amongst the Local 802 musicians that, "Union member Lenny Finz was a lawyer who made it all happen so quickly."

The auto parts host wanted to throw a party his snobbish guests could talk about. Somehow, he got his wish.

"IT'S A GREAT BAND YOUR HONOR"

Here's another story...

Bob White, a club date bandleader who played mostly at weddings and Bar Mitzvahs signed a contract to provide six musicians for a Bar Mitzvah party to be held on a certain date. Although Bob was neither a singer nor front man (he was a drummer), at the host's insistence, Bob promised he would personally appear at the function. As it was however, Bob received another job for the same date and signed a contract. It was not an unusual practice for a bandleader in that end of the business to receive more than one job for the same date. When that would happen, the leader would usually provide a substitute who would be the sub-leader.

When the date arrived, Bob opted to play the affair he had signed up after the first contract in which he stated he would appear personally. Regarding that job, Bob sent six musicians, one of whom had a fine singing voice in addition to being a good trumpet player. He was designated the sub-leader of the Bob White orchestra for that occasion.

Not seeing Bob at his party as promised, the host expressed disappointment and registered his complaint with the sub-leader, but said nothing further throughout the evening. The party was a huge success. Everyone enjoyed the music, with particular praise for the singer who was quite talented. In fact, the guests had such a grand time that they continued to dance well beyond the contracted hours of 9pm to 1am, requiring the host to keep the band for an additional two hours of overtime.

When the party ended and it was time to pay the sub-leader, the host refused, claiming that Bob White's failure to appear was a breach of contract and therefore should be stiffed.

Bob retained me and I brought suit against the host, claiming the band and singer provided were of excellent musical quality, that the guests loved the music as evidenced by their dancing for two hours beyond the contract time, and that the host suffered no damages whatsoever. I alleged further that his failure to pay for the services he received, would result in an unjust enrichment to him.

AND THE BAND PLAYED ON

The case came to trial before a judge without a jury. To prove my claim, I had Bob bring the musicians and singer who actually performed at the party. I then requested that the judge listen to the music so that he could decide for himself the quality of the band that Bob provided. Taken aback by such an unusual request, the judge hesitated, pondered, and then ruled, "Granted. You may proceed."

Within minutes, the musicians set up, including an electric piano, drums, and other instruments. They played, and the singer sang two or three songs. People and court personnel who were walking outside the courtroom and heard music coming from inside, came in, took seats and applauded after every song. In short order, as people came into the courtroom, every seat was occupied, and the smile on the Judge's face said it all.

When it was all over, the host grudgingly agreed to settle the full contract amount less a small percentage the judge requested we deduct for good will.

At the end, the judge called me to the side bar and said in a whisper, "Counselor, I've been a judge for almost twenty years but what you did was one of the most creative and amazing experiences I have had in the thousands of cases before me. Congratulations."

It didn't take long for the news to spread around to the Local 802 Musicians. Suddenly, calls were coming in at such a rate that I needed a larger office.

MY OFFICE RELOCATION TO QUEENS COUNTY

During the same period, I received a call from the president of the Queens County Bar Association who having heard that I had been a professional singer, wanted me to perform at the annual Christmas show its members put on. He said he would sponsor me for membership and urged me to move my office to Queens County since he knew I lived in Bayside, Queens. He even recommended the office building

I should select in Jamaica, Queens, since it was the hub for most of the lawyers practicing in the county. I agreed, moved to Jamaica, opened an attractive office, hired a law assistant and a full-time secretary. Joining the Queens County Bar Association, I then became a member of the cast for the Christmas show. In addition to lawyers in the cast, there were many sitting Queens County judges who participated as well. Most of the participants had the usual bar room voices. When they heard me sing, they were fractured. After all, I had made a living for many years from singing professionally.

Within a short time, I was invited to almost every function in the county where I would always be asked to sing. It was an out-front way for me to meet many Queens judges, elected officials, and other dignitaries. At the same time, I was building up a personal injury practice that had me in a Queens court almost every day. With my name becoming more popular, politics seemed to be a good match with my entertainment background.

MY ENTRY INTO POLITICS

I was induced by a public official to run in the primary for the New York State Senate in 1956. As a newcomer, I ran against an entrenched candidate and lost. But the "Finz" name was getting around. My reputation as a lawyer

and former professional entertainer were both gaining in popularity. It was that latter role that brought me to one of the most memorable experiences I had up to that time...

Familiar with my entertainment background, the Queens Democratic Party would constantly call upon me to organize rallies and big political blowouts. After a number of county and citywide campaigns in which I was actively involved, I was named the county campaign director in 1960, for the very charismatic Democratic candidate for the presidency of the United States. It was in that role that I was asked to organize a giant rally and to select the appropriate place for the blockbuster celebration. After tireless planning covering every detail, which also required meetings with campaign advance teams and security matters with the police and Secret Service, the massive event was held at Sunnyside Gardens in Long Island City, the largest venue in Queens County at the time.

The candidate for President of the United States was John F. Kennedy, who was already 2 1/2 hours late. Sunnyside Gardens was packed to capacity with more than four thousand in attendance. In addition, more than 10,000 people lined the streets outside where loud speakers had been installed to broadcast what was happening inside the hall. Since JFK was running so late, I had to keep the crowd entertained both inside and out. For 2 1/2 hours, I sang songs, told jokes, made speeches, and drew upon whatever show biz hoopla I had, just to keep the thousands who were waiting patiently for JFK occupied and entertained. It was a tough assignment.

When JFK finally arrived with his entourage and Secret Service, I was there to greet him at the door. His first question to me was, "Where's the john?" With his security detail all around, I rushed him into the nearest one. When I think back, it was an unforgettable and hilarious scene. There he was, John F. Kennedy, the future President of the United States, in front of a urinal with me standing right next to him. When finished, I escorted him quickly to the stage amidst the spirited music and the wild screams of the audience who were experiencing a great moment in history. I made a very brief introduction, ending with the traditional, "The next President of the United States, John F. Kennedy." There aren't enough adjectives to describe how fantastic he was to the thousands inside and outside the hall, whose enormous response showed their admiration and adulation. As for the rally, it was a rousing success. As for me, it was a breakout political opportunity.

MY CAMPAIGN SLOGAN
"LF/JFK YOUR PARTNERS FOR PROGRESS"

All the efforts I put into the big event were not without reward. Two years later in 1962, JFK, already being in office two years, assisted in getting me the nod as the Democratic candidate for the U.S. Congress. My admiration for JFK inspired my campaign slogan, "LF/JFK—Your Partners for Progress". President Kennedy also appointed me his Queens County spokesman to push for the Medicare bill which still had not become law. As to my candidacy to the House of Representatives, I faced a powerful incumbent and career politician. The congressional district in those days was still largely Republican, it having been gerrymandered to give an advantage to my opponent. It was an uphill battle and I lost.

Losing the election was not one of the greatest days of my life.

MY TRAVELS TO THE WHITE HOUSE

As a congressional candidate, however, I had made many visits to D.C., where on several occasions I had memorable conversations with JFK in the Rose Garden of the White House. To this day I still get chills as I treasure the time spent and pictures taken with the President of the United States. I also met with Secretary of State Dean Rusk who was most helpful in familiarizing me with some of the issues of foreign policy I would face on the campaign trail. In addition, JFK introduced me to his brother Robert, who, when he ran for the U.S. Senate in New York in 1964, had me named as his Queens County campaign director.

Who could have predicted that on November 22, 1963, the life of President John Fitzgerald Kennedy would come to such a tragic end. It was one of the saddest days for Americans and people around the world.

Back to Robert F. Kennedy... I organized a mammoth rally for RFK at a huge site upon which Rochdale Village in Queens was later developed. More than 15,000 people filled a vacant field as I introduced him to a wildly enthusiastic crowd. In fact, there was such a crush of people moving forward to gain a closer look at him, that the police and security detail were concerned that the portable stage that was brought in was in danger of being knocked over. Fortunately, the large police squad at the scene was able to control the adoring crowd. At the end, the rally was a huge success, the RFK experience for me being momentous at the time. He continued his charismatic campaign throughout New York State and defeated a strong Republican incumbent, Senator Kenneth Keating, who was running for a second term. Sadly, RFK was assassinated in California four years later. Another tragic day for America.

MY ELECTION AS NEW YORK CITY CIVIL COURT JUDGE

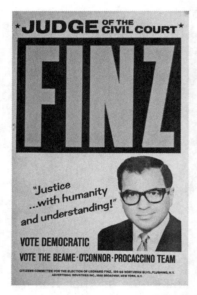

The following year, 1965, I became the Democratic candidate for Civil Court Judge of the City of New York in Queens County. The "Finz" name was fairly well known by this time as a result of all the high-level political, civic, and legal activities I was involved with. Consequently, I bagged the election by a good margin, learning later that when sworn in I was the youngest Civil Court Judge of New York City at the time. I was also the first in my NYU law school class to become a Judge.

During my judicial tenure, I was appointed a full adjunct professor of law at New York Law School in Manhattan, later receiving a teaching award from Warren Burger, the Chief Justice of the United States Supreme Court. Pretty cool.

But even the honor of becoming a Judge, or receiving an award from the Chief Justice, did not rise to being the greatest day of my life.

My meeting with President John F. Kennedy
in the Rose Garden of the White House, Washington, D.C. 1962.

With President Kennedy in one of my campaign posters for Congress. 1962.

One of my campaign bumper stickers. 1962.

I am appointed by President Kennedy to lead the fight for Medicare in Queens County. 1962.

I am appointed as the Queens Campaign Chairman by Robert F. Kennedy
who was a candidate for the United States Senate from New York.

I am conferring with Secretary of State Dean Rusk, on The Middle East crisis. 1962.

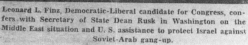

Leonard L. Finz, Democratic-Liberal candidate for Congress, confers with Secretary of State Dean Rusk in Washington on the Middle East situation and U. S. assistance to protect Israel against Soviet-Arab gang-up.

TESTIMONIAL DINNER
IN HONOR OF

Leonard L. Finz

DEMOCRATIC CANDIDATE FOR CONGRESS
6th C.D. QUEENS

LEONARD'S OF GREAT NECK

October 31, 1962

The cover page of the pamphlet setting out the testimonial dinner held in my honor when I ran for the U.S. House of Representatives. 1962.

My campaign slogan. 1962.

At one of my congressional campaign rallies. 1962.

I am in the center. To my left is Frank D. O'Connor, the Democratic candidate for governor of New York in 1966. To my right is Howard J. Samuels, the Democratic candidate for Lieutenant Governor on the O'Connor ticket.

A campaign card for New York City Civil Court Judge.
My qualifications appear on the rear of the card, on the right.

A campaign bumper sticker when I ran in the primary for the New York State Senate. 1956.

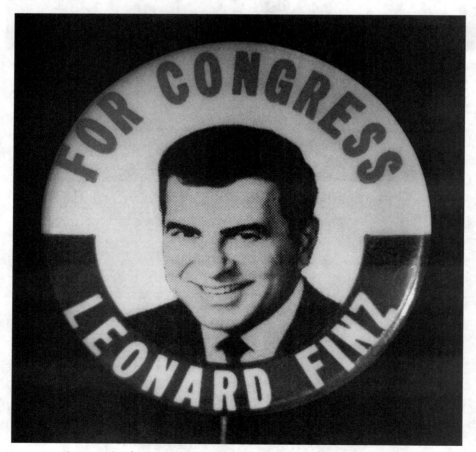

A campaign button when I ran for Unites States Congress. 1962.

One of my campaign posters when I ran for Judge of the New York City Civil Court. 1965.

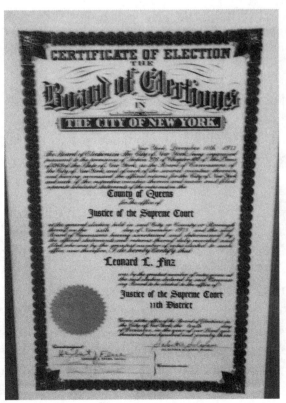

My official Certificate of Election as Justice of the Supreme Court, County of Queens, New York State.

MY BEING SELECTED TO ATTEND
THE NATIONAL JUDICIAL COLLEGE

THE NATIONAL
JUDICIAL COLLEGE

It was during the early months of 1971, when my Administrative Judge walked into my small chambers and asked, "How would you like to attend a new school for judges at the University of Nevada at Reno this summer?" Surprised, I asked, "What's it all about?" He responded, "It was organized last year with a federal grant and named the National Judicial College." I asked further, "What's the take, and where do I fit in?" In essence, he said it was the brainchild of a highly respected federal Circuit Court Judge who designed it to provide continuing judicial education for judges in every State of the Union. I asked, "What's the deal?" He said that each state would select a handful of special judges to attend for one month. That it would be a no-nonsense educational experience with courses starting at 8 am and finishing at 4:30 pm. That there'd be a dinner break from 5 pm to 6:30 pm, and that a workshop from 7pm to 9pm would be held every night. That it would be broken down into ten judge groups, each judge being from a different state. That the courses would cover a multitude of subjects conducted by judicial scholars and law professors from the finest schools in the country.

He added, that having been hand-picked to attend was an honor in itself, and that all expenses would be covered. "I think you should consider this most seriously," he added. "Sounds like a great idea, but since I would be away from my family for a whole month, I'll have to discuss it with my wife," I replied.

Pearl agreed that it was an opportunity I shouldn't pass up. With that, when summer came, I flew out to Reno and registered for the program at the National Judicial College. There were several hundred judges from the other states who registered at the same time. When registration was completed, we were all directed into a large auditorium and told to find seats. We were each handed a sheet of paper with the legend, "Sentencing Sheet". Within minutes, a rep of the judicial college took the stage and presented a brief description of the course we were about to start. He then discussed the "Sentencing Sheet" earlier handed out. What happened next was quite illuminating...

Looking straight at the audience, the rep said, "Soon, the auditorium lights will be turned off, and the large screen behind me will show a film that runs about fifteen minutes. Once the film is over, the lights will be switched back on, at which time you will write clearly on that sheet the sentence you would have imposed if you were the judge presiding in the case. In addition, you will set out the reasons supporting your decision."

This should be most fascinating, I thought. The lights were turned off and the movie started...

THE FIGHT IN THE POOLROOM

It began with two men in a poolroom. One was black, the other, white. They were shooting pool, eight ball to be exact, with a side bet of a few dollars. During the game, a dispute arose. Loud words became more intense as violent pushing and shoving took over. Within minutes there was a furious fistfight. Solid blows to the face and body were landed as the two fought fiercely. In the heat of battle, the black man grabbed a pool stick, and with a solid blow, struck the white man's head with the thick end with such violence as to knock him down hard, striking his head against a leg of the heavy pool table. Unconscious and bleeding heavily, he was spread out motionless on the poolroom floor. The white guy was dead.

The black man was charged with homicide, tried by a jury and found guilty. The next scene presented the criminal backgrounds of each. As for the dead white man, he had a record of two misdemeanors, a DUI, and an assault with a baseball bat upon a neighbor for which he served eleven months in a local jail. Regarding the black man found guilty of homicide, he had a record of domestic violence, petty shoplifting, and a felony conviction for burglary of a gun shop for which he served three years in a state prison. Of course, the two men in the film were professional actors.

THE SENTENCE TO BE IMPOSED

The judges in the audience now had to impose an appropriate sentence in addition to the reasons supporting it. Each of the several hundred judges began filling out the "Sentencing Sheet", as did I, after which all papers were collected. A recess was then called with the instruction to remain near the auditorium since we would have to return to our seats once the staff completed their tally.

Twenty minutes later, the same rep who oriented our group earlier, took the stage as we re-entered the auditorium and took our seats. Looking out to the audience, he said, "Our criminal justice system fails when there is an absence of standardized sentencing for the same crime. On that point, you all witnessed the same facts that ultimately resulted in a jury verdict of 'Guilty'. You also all read the criminal records of the two in the film. One would think that since each of you were selected by your own states to attend the National Judicial College because of your ability and reputation, the sentence you handed out on these sheets would be within a reasonably similar range." What followed, was an unbelievable shocker...

He continued, "Just listen to this. The sentence imposed on the black man in the film, ranged from probation... to... execution, and everything in between." The gasp of surprise from the judges in the auditorium said it all. "And this is further proof of the great disparity and injustice that can accompany the punishment meted out by judges of experience and good will. That is one of the reasons you are here. Many of our courses will focus upon fair and just standards for sentencing procedures. This most important part of criminal justice reform will be thoroughly discussed and dealt specifically in several of your evening workshop sessions."

To me, what I had just witnessed was an eye-opener and a chilling introduction to the many courses and judicial issues to be covered in the one-month intensive course to follow.

During the next thirty days, we received the most enlightened judicial thinking from scholars on subjects ranging from, judicial temperament, judicial discretion, constitutional law, evidence, criminal procedure, just to name a few. Within a month, having exchanged views with hundreds of judges throughout the country, I completed the program and received an official certificate. I like to think I came away from that rewarding experience a better judge to those who appeared in my courtroom, and who looked to me for those three powerful words, "justice", "fairness", and "courtesy".

A WORKSHOP THAT WENT TERRIBLY WRONG

On the human-interest side, there's an intriguing and shocking story I must relate...

A highly respected faculty member headed a workshop on criminal justice reform. When the class ended at 9pm, one judge persuaded a colleague in the group to go to a gin mill within a ten-minute walk from the college campus just to unwind from a busy day. When they arrived, they sat at the bar. Within five minutes, a young couple, he in his 30's, and she, an attractive young woman of about the same age also sat at the bar. The female occupied the seat next to one of the judges.

Within a few minutes, the voices of the two-young people got louder. It was obvious they were in a heated argument that was escalating in intensity. From time to time, the judge seated next to the young woman turned his head toward them recognizing that their heated words were becoming more hostile. As anger rose, the young man started to push his female partner viciously. Seeing this, the judge, not willing to just stand by and witness a young woman being abused, got in the middle trying to calm things down. He told the young man to "cool it" and to keep his hands off the young woman. Not taking kindly to the judge's intrusion, the young man reached over and in anger, struck the judge with a hard blow to his left shoulder. That aggressive action resulted in the two of them wrestling with each other and exchanging blows. The other judge just stood on the side with an uncertain look on his face.

Several police who were in a fast food joint next door heard the commotion and rushed into the gin mill. They broke up the fight and after a few words with the young man, put the cuffs, not on him, but on the judge. The judge was arrested and forcefully whisked out to the patrol car outside despite the judge's protestations that he did not start the fight. He also kept repeating in a panicked voice that he was a judge attending the National Judicial College. The cops responded by handling him roughly with repeated warnings to "shut your goddam mouth."

The judge was taken to the police precinct several blocks away, booked, fingerprinted, photographed, and tossed into an empty cell with neither chair nor bench. For the next hour, he pleaded with the police and demanded that he wanted to contact the judicial college. He was warned over and over again to, "shut the f**k up or things will get a lot worse." Callously, he was told to tell it to the arraignment judge in the morning.

Having no choice, he slumped down to the floor, his back against the wall. With hands on his knees cupping his bowed head, he remained silent and sat there bewildered, not knowing what would happen to him next.

The news had gotten out to the press that a judge had been arrested for "fighting over a woman" in a local bar. Within a half hour, photographers were allowed into the precinct. They took pictures of the judge through the bars of the jail cell of him sitting on the floor.

The next morning, the judge was removed from his cell under guard, and with handcuffs around his wrists, was escorted into a small courtroom to be arraigned. When his name was called, he stood before the judge and started to speak. His voice was filled with emotion but before he could even get through a sentence, he was abruptly cut off. What happened next was the real shocker...

Smiling and with a benign voice that came from the arraignment judge, he was told that the whole episode was a planned hoax designed by the judicial college faculty member who taught criminal procedure. That everyone involved, from the other judge who invited him to the bar, to the bartender, the young man and his female partner, to the arresting police, and everyone else, were all acting a part. The whole purpose it was explained, was for the "victim" judge to relate to the other judges in the class, the pain, agony, and frustrations of a citizen who was wrongly accused. And how some defendants were treated after being arrested. The underlying purpose of the "hoax" was intended to provide a more sensitive understanding of a helpless defendant who stood before them in the criminal court.

Although well intended as a teaching tool, the difficulty with the "hoax" demonstration was that the photos taken of the judge sitting on the floor in a jail cell, appeared on the front page of his hometown newspapers. It also included the sordid details of his arrest as a result of a fight he had in a bar. The "hoax" angle was left out of the original published story. Despite corrections later printed to describe his being a "victim" of a judicial college experiment, the photographic image of the judge (who had a wife and children) in a jail cell, and a physical fight in a gin mill that "involved a young woman" was to remain his legacy. He also had to explain to his wife what he was doing in a saloon in the first place. As for his children of school age, they had to suffer the riding that other kids have such fun in dishing out.

The Board of Directors of the National Judicial College was so outraged at the misguided plan (despite its beneficial intent), that the faculty member who dreamed it up was discharged, and never invited back. Although the concept was a novel one, it was viewed as an exercise of poor judgment, and an unfair blight upon the good standing of the targeted victim who spent the balance of his judicial career as the butt of painful and insensitive jokes.

MY APPOINTMENT AS FACULTY MEMBER AND OTHER HONORS

Years later, I was invited by the college to return, not as a student since I was no longer on the bench, but as a member of the faculty. I accepted, the teaching commitment being for only two weeks over the summer. Describing the courses I taught, I instructed many of the student judges in the use of special courtroom techniques that could be employed in adversarial trials in very hotly contested cases. In addition,  I also offered judicial seminars on forensic medical issues since many judges (mostly in rural areas) were unfamiliar with medical malpractice cases that were first beginning to surface.

I was invited again as a faculty member for several summers thereafter, receiving a special teaching certificate at the end of my last teaching season.

An award was also presented to me by the Dean of the National Judicial College when I was honored as "Man of the Year" by The Federation of Jewish Philanthropies at what was then described as the largest attendance then recorded for such a Queens County event. It was a dinner that was held at the Terrace on the Park, one of the historic buildings erected for the 1964-1965 World's Fair. The main speaker was Governor Mario Cuomo, a former Queens County Bar Association member and friend.

But even with the honors that included the "Man of the Year" award, the Dean's National Judicial College presentation, Governor Cuomo's laudatory comments, and the large attendance, they did not, all combined, measure up to the greatest day of my life.

MY BEING THE FOUNDER OF
THE BRANDEIS ASSOCIATION

I was a New York City Civil Court Judge for only two years when it struck me that although there were many ethnic professional organizations throughout the state, city, and county of Queens (with a population of almost two million), there was no organization that dealt solely with lawyers of the Jewish faith. The year was 1968, anti-Semitism was a serious issue, Israel was surrounded by enemies and had just survived a war with Egypt and Syria. In addition, there were many issues that affected the Jewish community at large.

Prior to World War II, Queens County had but a handful of Jewish residents as compared to either Brooklyn or the Bronx. After the war, a huge influx came into Queens searching out the new garden apartment complexes and apartment buildings that made developers drool with financial delight.

More Jewish lawyers were suddenly signing office leases in such areas as Jamaica, Forest Hills, Kew Gardens, and Flushing. But unlike other ethnic groups, there was no organization exclusively of Jewish lawyers.

With that knowledge, I enlisted my dear friend Bernie Hirschhorn who became the second member of the new organization I just created. As history records, I enlisted the assistance of the Long Island Press and its owner, SI Newhouse, in addition to the most respected Jewish leader in the county, Rabbi Israel Moshowitz. The highest political Queens County officer, Borough President Donald Manes, and the most influential Jewish lawyers in the county together with a handful of my colleagues on the bench, were also an integral part of the effort.

I even gave the name to the new organization, calling it the "Brandeis Association", named after Louis Brandeis, the first Jewish Justice ever named to the United State Supreme Court.

The organizing effort was enormous and tedious in which the association continued to grow in size and stature throughout the state, city, and county. Most new organizations cease to exist after a few months. In fact, within several years after its birth, a number of Jewish judges and lawyers became members, many of whom served on its board of directors.

After six years as its Chairman of the Board, I yielded the seat to Supreme Court Justice Nat Hentel, secure that the Brandeis Association was on a strong path.

ELECTED LIFETIME
HONORARY CHAIRMAN OF THE BOARD

My efforts as the "Founder" were rewarded by my being elected to the lifetime position of "Honorary Chairman of the Board" at an official ceremony in which I was presented with a large portrait and plaque I proudly hang on the wall of my home.

The Brandeis Association has defied all odds by having grown where at the present, almost fifty years after it was born, it is one of the most respected and reputable professional organizations in the State of New York, the city, and county of Queens. In fact, its membership includes talented attorneys, judges, office holders and community leaders. I am extremely honored that my dream of half a century ago has grown to be the exceptional and powerful organization it is today.

Although the day I became the "Founder" of the Brandeis Association fills me with a special pride, it still does not rise to being the greatest day of my life.

MY MEETING WITH DONALD TRUMP

Having been extremely active in Queens politics and community affairs, I was appointed Urban Renewal Chairman by Borough President Pat Clancy, served as Chairman of the Eagle Scout Board, and participated actively in many other top civic roles. Being a public figure, my wife and I would often attend many fund-raisers and functions sponsored by the city and county organizations with which I was actively involved.

It was at one of the dinners where I sat at the same table with Fred Trump, the largest developer of homes and apartment complexes in Brooklyn and Queens at the time. In fact, he and his family were constituents of mine, having a large home on Midland Parkway in Jamaica Estates, that was within the district in which I ran for Justice of the Supreme Court.

I met his son Donald sometime after the 1964-1965 World's Fair held in Queens. When the Fair ended, one of its buildings was used as a theatre named the "Queens Playhouse", where Broadway-styled musicals and plays were performed. That is where we were first introduced. I would also see Trump at various functions from time to time where we would often engage in small talk.

It was some time in the 1980's when he and his wife Ivana invited my wife Pearl and me to the Trump Castle, one of his new casino hotels in Atlantic City, New Jersey. We accepted their VIP invitation and found the hotel pleasant enough. Sometime in 1985, we were invited to a special cocktail party held at the Trump Tower, a fifty-eight-story glass structure he built on the site of the old Bonwit-Teller building on Fifth Avenue between 56th and 57th Street in Manhattan. Construction of the Tower began in 1979 and was completed in 1983. Hearing much about Trump Tower, we decided to attend.

At the party, Trump pitched his Atlantic City Hotels in the glitzy lobby where the festivities were being held. It was there I engaged him in a brief conversation which dealt mostly with our Queens roots and his parents' Jamaica Estates home, which was just several blocks from the supreme court building located on Sutphin Boulevard. It was where I had presided prior to my resigning from the bench.

While at the cocktail party, Trump also invited us to his Mar-a-Lago estate in Palm Beach, not as overnight guests, but for a special tour of his Florida showplace. We thanked him, but declined the invitation.

Subsequently, we were invited several times to the Trump Castle in Atlantic City which appealed to us, since it was located on the marina side, and not clustered with the other casino hotels on the Atlantic side of the boardwalk.

Several stories stick out which bear telling...

TRUMP SAYS
"YOU'RE THE BEST PUBLIC SPEAKER IN QUEENS"

Having been invited as VIP guests, we were escorted to a nice suite. At the entrance table there was a black box with the Trump Castle name engraved on a brass plate. When we opened the box, it contained an array of imported fragrances, powders, shaving materials, and other attractive little gifts.

There also was a printed welcoming message, together with a handwritten invitation from Ivana and Donald Trump, to attend an afternoon rehearsal of a fashion show scheduled to be held that evening in the showroom.

After settling in, we proceeded to the rehearsal area. Trump at the time was involved with others, but came over when he saw us enter the showroom. Looking directly at Pearl, he said, "I've heard him a number of times. In my book, your husband is the best public speaker in Queens County." It was an extremely high compliment coming from someone who one day would become the 45th President of the United States.

THE ASHTRAY IS CEMENTED TO THE TABLE

Another Donald Trump story...

On one of our VIP visits, we were provided with a huge, nicely decorated suite. It was so large that there even was an oversized, ornate Jacuzzi, not in the bathroom, but in the spacious bedroom itself. Looking around the suite, Pearl and I both agreed that the Trumps seemed to know how to do things right. There was an ordinary looking ashtray on top of one of the tables. I attempted to move it so that I could make room for some items I was emptying from my pockets. To my surprise, the ashtray could not be moved. To my further surprise, it had been cemented, yes, cemented, to the table's surface. Pearl and I looked at each other, shrugged, and had a good laugh over it. But despite the cemented ash tray caper, Trump Castle was an Atlantic City hotel we always preferred.

A post script: On November 8, 2016, Donald Trump was elected president of the United States. Will he serve the highest office in the nation within traditional presidential boundaries and protocols or will he reign as king of the castle? Time will tell.

MY PLAN TO ABC-TV FOR A
NEW SHOW CALLED "THE JUDGE"

I was a New York City Civil Court Judge sitting in my small chambers in Kew Gardens, Queens, when a TV idea came to me. Considering all the human-interest cases I had dealt with, and the insight that developed through my courtroom dealings with so many litigants and lawyers, I created a format for a TV series I named "The Judge". Since I had a dear friend, Bernard Hirschhorn, who had a strong connection with a vice president of a major TV network, I asked if he could arrange a

meet with the exec so that I could present my idea as a new TV show.

Arrangements were made, and we did meet with him, at which time I presented my format setting out the cast of characters together with a story board containing 13 different plot themes. The TV exec appeared most enthusiastic and said he would give the matter serious consideration. I never heard from him, not again, directly, anyway.

One year following our meeting, his network "coincidentally" featured a new TV series, called, "The Judge". It starred Tony Randall in the role. I watched the series most carefully and recognized that several of the plot themes I had presented a year before were contained in several of the shows.

Outraged that a TV idea that I presented to a major TV network executive was in essence stolen from me, my friend and I engaged a prominent boutique Manhattan law firm to bring an action against the network. In its defense, the network hired one of the hot shot elite white shoe Wall Street firms.

For years, they strategically delayed the case and dragged everything out. They drowned us with so many paper motions and technical nonsense (a typical Wall Street law firm strategy), to the point where we could no longer afford the legal costs to continue the litigation. Reluctantly, we had to abandon the suit.

The entire TV "Judge" experience was most disappointing with a result that did not add up to the greatest day of my life.

MY ANNUAL SUPER BOWL PARTY

For several years, Richard A. Brown, the present District Attorney of Queens County; Seymour Boyers, a retired Associate Justice of the Appellate Division, Second Department; and the late Councilman Donald Manes, who later became Borough President; and I, would play doubles at a tennis facility. Our seasonal tennis game would be held on a Sunday from 11am to 1pm.

On this occasion, it was February 1976, Super Bowl Day, the earlier games did not attract the massive interest of the future extravaganzas.

After our tennis match, while changing in the locker room, I mentioned casually that, "Today is Super Bowl Day. Why don't you guys come over to the house. I'll grab some deli sandwiches on the way and some beer and we can watch the game." They thought it a good idea and said they'd come over around a half hour before game time.

When I arrived home, Pearl and I drew some banners on oaktag I had in the house, printing the names of the teams on them. We then scotch-taped them to the wall of the den where one of the TVs was located and put out some chips and nuts. This was the start of our first Super Bowl party.

The next year, I invited a few of my judge colleagues in addition to my three tennis partners. I repeated the party each year, enlarging the number of guests, being more lavish in our decorations, food, and drink.

By 1997, almost twenty years later, I had invited many more colleagues, legislators, and neighbors; setting up TV's in my den, living room, dining room; and even hired a bartender. By this time, the number attending my annual Super Bowl party had swelled to more than 40 guests. Pearl took care of the decorations and little gifts we gave out. Each Super Bowl party was larger and more successful than the year before. In fact, it was so popular that a number of judges who had not previously been on the guest list wanted to attend the next Super Bowl party that Lenny Finz would throw.

That year, in 1997, we sold our house in Little Neck, Queens, and purchased a home within a gated community called "Gracewood". It had once been the estate of a shipping magnate in the 1930's. Located within the community was the original mansion with its large ceremonial main salon. It was there that every Finz Super Bowl party was held each year thereafter with the addition that our guest list grew accordingly.

By 2013, thirty-seven years after I hosted three of my tennis buddies with deli sandwiches and beer, I had a guest list of almost 100 men (the maximum the salon could hold), who attended my annual Super Bowl party.

With the creative supervision of Pearl, my son Stuart, who for the last few years shared the hosting job with me, in addition to an employee of my son's law firm (Finz & Finz), Bill Van Roten, a retiree of the NYPD; the Finz annual Super Bowl party became the prestige "talk about" event of the year in which Supreme Court Justices, Congressmen, State and City legislators, and others attended.

THE GROWTH OF THE SUPER BOWL PARTY

Growing from the years leading up to 2013, we now had three valets to park cars; the delivery of 25 tables and 100 chairs delivered to the mansion on the Friday before the big game; and a crew of five who moved all the furniture out of the grand salon and set up the tables and chairs. In addition, they set up a large bar.

On Super Bowl Sunday morning, a decorating crew would transform the mansion, and especially the grand salon, with hundreds of balloons, signs, life size cardboard football stars, goal posts, and hundreds of pennants I had collected from previous Super Bowl events.

When finished, the entire motif within the grand salon made it look like a football stadium.

At 1pm, two engineers would set up a huge screen covering one entire wall of the grand salon in addition to the installation of a high-tech sound system. At 2pm, six waiters from Pearl's East, the best Asian restaurant on the North Shore, would arrive and set out red tablecloths and centerpieces on each table. They would then proceed to an adjourning room (the library) where they would set up long tables, stack plates, and put out the silverware for the lavish buffet that would include a variety of Asian food during the halftime dining period.

On the day before the game, we would prepare the following: Gift bags containing a Super Bowl hat, a Super Bowl ski cap, a Super Bowl T-shirt, a Super Bowl long sleeve sweatshirt, a gift box containing a man's cologne, and a large box of Valentine chocolates to bring home to the guest's spouse.

In addition, there would be two bartenders and two greeters at the door entrance who would distribute the gift bags to guests upon their arrival and carry their coats to another room of the mansion where racks would have been set up.

The guests would usually begin to arrive between 4pm and 5pm (game time was at 6:30 pm) during which time appetizers would be served, and with an open bar throughout the game. At 6pm, when most guests were already seated, Stuart and I would give out door prizes (I would have been collecting them all year). In addition, we would present, "Man of the Year" trophies that resembled the Heisman Trophy to several guests in a ten-minute ceremony. Each trophy would already have a brass plate inscribed with the name of the honoree.

In addition to everything else, we would have a photograph booth where individual souvenir pictures would be taken and could be printed upon a T-shirt, a popular magazine cover, or in a group with famed sports figures, etc. We would also have a roving artist to draw quick caricatures of a guest, placing the art work in a printed frame with the legend, "Finz Super Bowl Party", and the date. At times, we even had Cuban cigar makers rolling handmade cigars from large tobacco leaves with each cigar band being imprinted, "Compliments of the Finz Super Bowl Party".

During half-time, each guest would proceed to the next room, the library, and fill up his plate with piping hot delicious Asian food being served by six waiters and a chef.

The proprietor of Pearl's East would also arrange for a most attractive sushi table. She would come by several times, stay awhile to ensure that everything was coming off as planned, and was always dressed in a beautifully styled flowered long kimono. When there, I would take the microphone in hand, and say, "Folks, this is Kathy, the owner of Pearl's East, the finest restaurant on the North Shore."

Judges, legislators, and other guests, would be casual, let their hair down and react with screams when their team scored an important play. It was a blast to see, hear, and witness such uninhibited fun in its fullest posture.

When the game would be over, the same crew that removed the furniture from the grand salon the morning before, would return, and within three hours would clean up and return the furniture to its original spot. When finished, no one would ever know that a huge party had just been held.

We ran the "Finz Annual Super Bowl Party" every year for 37 years straight and finally discontinued it in 2013, to everyone's disappointment. But as it is often said, "All good things at some point must come to an end." And in the case of the "Finz Super Bowl Party", the end had come.

What is most astonishing, however, is that not a single one of the 37 Super Bowl Parties, although always held on the first Sunday of February (the height of winter) was ever snowed out. Indeed, the weather was always perfect. It's almost as if someone up there was looking down upon us, throwing a benevolent wink, and saying, "Okay, guys. Have a great time."

Some of the decorations at the Finz annual Super Bowl party.

FIRED UP~ READY TO GO!!!

to the TRADITIONAL FINZ 37TH ANNUAL SUPER BOWL XLVII Party

Sunday, February 3, 2013 at 4:30pm

The Mansion at Gracewood
41 Shelter Rock Road, Manhasset, New York
RSVP to Ashley (516) 433-3000

The invitation to the 37th annual Super Bowl party which was the final one we held.

The entrance to the Gracewood mansion where Super Bowl hats, gift bags, pennants, and decorations, were on display at one of the big parties.

Super Bowl prizes and souvenirs, in addition to gift bags containing a Super Bowl hat, t-shirt, sweatshirt, cologne, box of chocolates, which gifts were presented to our guests.

A cigar specialist making handmade cigars with a special ring band that stated, "Hand Rolled at the Finz Super Bowl Party."

A typical Super Bowl caricature of each guest (this one is of me), a photo booth, and other football novelties.

Our two congenial bartenders.

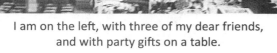

I am on the left, with three of my dear friends, and with party gifts on a table.

I am holding the mic for the Honorable Randall T. Eng, who later became the Presiding Justice of the Appellate Division, Second Judicial Department, New York. Justice Eng is presented with the Super Bowl "Man of the Year" trophy award (fashioned after the Heisman Trophy). Former Appellate Division Justice Seymour Boyers looks on approvingly.

I am with the Honorable Jeremy S. Weinstein, the Administrative Judge of the Supreme Court, Civil Division, Queens County, State of New York.

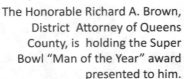

The Honorable Richard A. Brown, District Attorney of Queens County, is holding the Super Bowl "Man of the Year" award presented to him.

The Honorable Seymour Boyers, former Justice of the Appellate Division, Second Department, State of New York, is holding the Super Bowl "Man of the Year" award presented to him.

The Honorable Milton Mollen, Deputy Mayor of the City of New York, and former Presiding Justice of the Appellate Division, Second Judicial Department, addressing the large assemblage at a Super Bowl party. District Attorney Richard A. Brown, and I, are looking on.

Many of the guests at a Super Bowl party are watching the large TV screen in front of them.

Enjoying sushi as appetizers before the big halftime Super Bowl dinner.

This is at one of our earlier Super Bowl parties held in my home in which there were only a handful of guests in attendance.

MY HIGH-LOW CONTRACT WHERE BOTH SIDES WIN

As a judge handling hundreds of accident cases, I found that a verdict that would exceed the insurance coverage of a defendant could have a financially devastating effect upon him or her personally. In such an event, a house could be lost, life savings could be depleted, salaries could be garnished, and much more.

Conversely, if the injured plaintiff lost, it could impact heavily upon his or her future financial security, and other negative consequences.

With those conflicting possibilities, I wrote an article titled, "The High-Low Contract—Where Both Sides Win".

To describe briefly what it was... I would negotiate a deal where both sides agreed that in the event of a plaintiff's verdict, an agreed specific sum would be within the insurance policy limits, thereby protecting the individual defendant from financial destruction that could be faced. That agreed sum, would be the "High". It would also be agreed that if there was a defendant's verdict, the plaintiff could recover a specific, but lower sum. That, would be the "Low".

EVEN IF YOU LOSE YOU WIN

As an example...

Assuming the insurance policy covering a defendant driver was $100,000.00, a verdict in excess of that amount would have to be paid by the defendant personally, and could have a crushing impact on whatever assets were owned. As for the plaintiff, no verdict is guaranteed, and even what appears to be the strongest of cases, could be found otherwise by a jury. Thus, the parties, after negotiation with a judge, could enter into a "High-Low Contract" where in the event of a plaintiff's verdict, it would be in the agreed sum of the "High" (for example, $80,000). And in the event of a defendant's verdict, the sum of the "Low" would be applied (for example $20,000). Thus, both sides would reach a compromise, and at the end, both are virtual winners.

As for the injury, the role of the jury would be limited to returning a verdict on liability only, without reporting any amount. Enormous trial time would thereby be saved since no medical witnesses, economists, life planners, etc., would be necessary since the trial would focus solely upon who was at fault, and not on damages. Further, there would be no appeals, saving much time and money in eliminating the appellate process.

I presented the "High-Low Contract" concept to the Judicature Society, a highly reputable national organization, and submitted a supporting article that was published. That was more than forty years ago. In fact, my "High-Low" approach has been adopted in almost every state in the nation, with varying modifications, and is used constantly in trials throughout the country even to this day.

While I am extremely proud of that accomplishment, it still does not rise to being the greatest day of my life.

MY CLOSE-UP TO BIG NYC FIRES
WITH THE FIRE COMMISSIONER

One of the nicest men I had come across was Ed Thompson, an attorney. We first met at a parent-teachers' night at the private school attended by his daughter, my daughter and son. My wife and I made the move to a private school since the public school my kids had been attending was in total disarray as was the entire New York City Public School System at the time. Ensuring their safety, together with a meaningful education, meant everything to us. It was also a great sacrifice since the private school was costly, and my financial means were at low tide.

Having become a Civil Court Judge at such a young age, I had little opportunity to have earned enough to stash away anything for future financial security. Although my judge's salary was a respectful $25,000 per year, the taking out for full Federal, State, City, Social Security, Medical, and other taxes, left me with less than half of the gross. Paying a monthly mortgage, insurance, repairs, auto, food, household, and miscellaneous expenses, there was little, if anything, left. I even had to re-finance my mortgage. But as concerned parents, we wanted to do everything we could for our children.

Speaking with Ed and his wife that evening, we learned that their daughter was taking saxophone lessons. That opened-up a discussion when I told them I had been a professional sax man in my earlier years. "Do you think you could come over to the house some evening and listen to my daughter? Perhaps you could give her a few pointers." I said, "I'd be happy to."

Within the week we made the arrangements, and I visited Ed and his wife for the purpose of appraising their daughter's musical talent. I also brought my own sax along to have it, if needed.

Their daughter had been taking lessons for several years. She played a few exercises, after which they waited for my critique. I passed along some suggestions and spent 15 or 20 minutes in assisting her with tone and technique.

After thanking me and seeing that I had brought my sax along, they asked me to play something. Having been a professional musician, I opened with full tone scales and played one of the popular standards. They were overwhelmed by the sound and brilliance of my alto sax. When finished, I turned to their daughter and said, "You can play and sound like that, but it takes practice, practice, and more practice."

My wife and I made several visits to their home after that, and a close relationship was developed. I didn't know at the time that Ed had been a former high ranking fireman and a very close friend of Mayor Robert F. Wagner Jr. I was pleasantly surprised when I learned that the mayor had appointed him to be the Fire Commissioner of New York City.

BIG FIVE ALARMER

It was in that role that Ed telephoned me one evening. "Len, big fire downtown. How would you like to come along with me? Want me to pick you up?" "You bet," I answered excitedly. Within 10 minutes, a red vehicle with its lights, bells and whistles pulled into my driveway in Little Neck, Queens, and off we went. A trip that would normally take 45 minutes to an hour or more, took less than 20 minutes, given the siren, and a very aggressive driver.

Ed was a good friend and knew that my seeing what hero firefighters faced, would be an inspirational thrill and an unprecedented experience. To this day, I remember every detail, the roaring fire shooting out of the burning building, the belching up of thick, black smoke, the actions and skill of the brave firefighters, and the thrill of just being so close to the action.

I must have gone to a half dozen major fires at the side of Fire Commissioner Ed Thompson, my fire-fighting tour guide. I'll never forget how proud I felt watching our firefighters perform so tirelessly, while standing next to my dear friend, Commissioner Ed, who later became a New York State Supreme Court Justice.

As remarkable as the unique experiences were, there was still not one that rose to being the greatest day of my life.

MY BECOMING A NEW YORK STATE SUPREME COURT JUSTICE

After serving eight years as a Civil Court Judge, I received the nomination to the New York State Supreme Court. Being elected a Supreme Court Justice was no contest, considering I had the nomination of the three major political parties.

As one enters the beautiful marble-floored lobby of the historic Supreme Court building, there are elevators to the left. Above the left most elevator, is the name of, "Hon. Leonard L. Finz, Justice of the Supreme Court, 1974".

Taking the elevator to the second floor, you are led out into an enormous marbled area in which many of the courtrooms are located. Surrounding the floor's perimeter and about six feet above, are large 30x40 portraits of Supreme Court Justices who served in that majestic courthouse. One of the portraits is that of, "Supreme Court Justice Leonard L. Finz", an image that will remain there long after I am gone. My son Stuart and granddaughter Jackie have told me so many times how they admire the portrait when they are in the courthouse, and the pride they feel in seeing their black-robed father and grandfather almost immortalized by being part of such an imposing building that has stood there in almost its pristine form for more than eight decades.

But even being sworn in to such a high judicial position at such an early age, imposing portrait and all, does not rise to being the greatest day of my life.

THANKS FOR THE MEMORY

Sometime in the 1970s when I was still a judge, I received a call from the president of Queens College of the City University of New York (CUNY). He had heard me at one of the seminars I would often hold on different subjects and asked if I would be willing to join the adjunct faculty as a full professor and teach two courses. One was Business Law to graduating day time students for three hours each Saturday morning. The other was a course of my choice to be given under the ACE program – a specially crafted program designed for the mature students whose college was interrupted for personal or family reasons many years before. Gaining sufficient college credits under the ACE program would ultimately earn them a B.A. degree from the university.

Since I always enjoyed teaching, I agreed, and developed a course for the ACE program titled, "Law in Response to Social Change." The essence of the three-credit course was to teach how law did not evolve in a vacuum, but was a continuing response to the needs of a society. I prepared a syllabus, presented it to the president of the college who was fascinated by the unique concept, and gave his approval that the course be included in its bulletin for the coming semester. And here's the fascinating story that follows...

The class enrollment was limited to 35 ACE matriculated students and was filled on the first day. Meeting them for the first time, I noted that they were between the ages of 35 and 55. They were extremely motivated, and developed a quick comradery with each other. On varying assignments, I would have each of them act as prosecutor, defense counsel, witness, judge, and jury, on very pressing social issues. The roles from time to time were changed. The discussion periods were always intelligent, lively, and provocative.

Since it was a three-hour class from 7pm to 10pm, there would be a short break in the middle, with coffee and cake supplied each week from very willing students. It is noteworthy, and indeed a testimonial, that no one ever missed a class.

As part of the Kumbaya spirit, I would at times arrange to meet with the class at 6pm at a local eatery and then proceed to the Queens College campus to begin class at 7pm. I even had several field trips to the Kew Gardens, Queens, Criminal Court House where members of the class could witness night criminal court arraignments and other court procedures. As a result of my judicial position, every courtesy was extended by the court personnel, in addition to short discussions had with the judge actually presiding.

The enthusiasm of the class, and their desire to discuss the intricacies and nuances of, "Law and Society," were immeasurable. When the term came to an end, they threw me a surprise party and presented me with a 20 x 30 hand scripted plaque they designed, which each class member signed. It hangs proudly in my study at home.

The theme of the plaque was, "Thanks for the memory," the words of which follow:

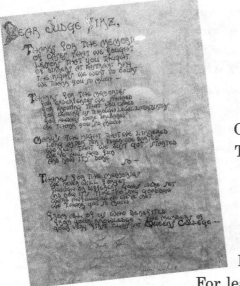

Dear Judge Finz

Thanks for the memories
Of cases that we fought
Lessons that you taught
Of dinners at Pastrami King
The nights we went to court
We thank you so much

Thanks for the memories
For experiences we shared
For knowing that you cared
For leading us through legal labyrinths
You always were prepared
We thank you so much

Many's the night that we lingered
Long after ten, then we parted
We felt that we just got started
We've all had fun and now it's done – so

Thanks for the memories
We never will forget
Though on different goals we're set
We're awfully glad we've met
We thank you so much

———

From all of us who benefitted from your knowledge -
the members of your very first class at Queens College
(The above was signed by every member of the class)

Teaching those in their middle age who were so desirous of obtaining a college degree was an indescribable joy for me. Coincidentally, several years ago, a gentleman approached me at a wedding who told me he had been in my class at Queens College. He heaped much praise upon me, stressing that the course I presented gave him a perspective that assisted him greatly throughout his life. I felt extremely proud of that. But even with all of the pleasure, and pride, I felt in making some contribution to each members journey of knowledge, it did not add up to the greatest day of my life.

MY PLAYING TENNIS ON THE
CENTER COURT OF THE U.S. TENNIS OPEN

How many weekend tennis hackers can ever say they played at Arthur Ashe Stadium, center court for the U.S. Open, a court that through the years has been glorified with such great tennis immortals as Federer, Nadal, Agassi, Evert, Navratilova, and many more? Well, I can. For many seasons, former New York State Appellate Division Justice Seymour Boyers, former Bronx Supreme Court Administrative Judge Burton Roberts, Queens District Attorney Richard A. Brown, and I, had booked two hours of doubles each Sunday morning at the U.S. Open public courts.

One Sunday morning in October, when the weather was still mild, District Attorney Brown told us he had a big surprise. He had arranged for us to play on the main center stadium court of the U.S. Open, a court that had never been open to the public. Wow. We were all floored and in great anticipation as we hurriedly walked the long distance from the public courts onto the hallowed U.S. Open Championship Stadium Court. What a thrill that was. We played our usual hacking doubles game, surrounded by 20,000 empty seats.

Although it was an extraordinary experience, it still was not the greatest day of my life.

1965, being sworn in as a New York City Civil Court Judge.

Making a point while in chambers.

NEW YORK LAW SCHOOL

Leonard L. Finz

Adjunct Professor of Law

In Recognition of your 5 Years of
Distinguished Service to the Scholastic Excellence
of the Law School and the Profession

June 10, 1984

Award for service as a New York
Law School Professor of Law.

On the bench in my courtroom.

Editorial
published by
the New York
Daily News.

DAILY NEWS
Queens

Donald Bertrand, Queens Regional Editor. Queens editorial offices: 116-16 Queens Blvd., Forest Hills, 11375, Telephone (212) 793-7272.

GOOD WORK, JUDGE

For many years two neighbors on 87th St. in Ozone Park had not talked to one another—a cold relationship made even colder by the fact that King, the German shepherd owned by one of the men, allegedly bit the other man three times.

After the third bite, an execution order was issued for King under the city Health Code. His owner protested to Jamaica Supreme Court, submitting petitions signed by more than 500 names attesting to King's "gentle temperament and his fondness for children."

The case went before Justice Leonard L. Finz (himself the owner of a Scottish terrier) who saw the legalities to the basic issue: "The root of the problem appears to be not that the dog doesn't get along with people but that the people don't along with each other."

Whereupon, he persuaded the two neighbors to shake hands and speak to each other. He also spared King's life, but prudently ordered his owner to erect a six-foot-high fence to keep King in his own yard.

Isn't it refreshing to find a judge who can rule with his heart as well as his head?

My being presented with a portrait for service as Founder and Chairman of the Board of The Brandeis Association. Circa 1974.

The plaque honoring me as the Founder and Chairman of the Board of The Brandeis Association.

My "High-Low" article published nationally in Judicature magazine.

One of my press photos.

One of my campaign materials for Judge of the New York City Civil Court. 1965.

Citation of Honor presented by The Brandeis Association

The judges of the NYC Civil Court. I was the youngest judge elected at the time.

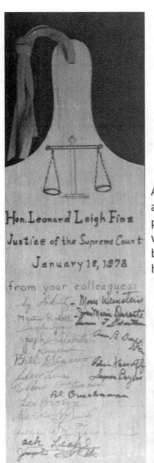

The portrait of me on display at the New York State Supreme Court courthouse in Jamaica, Queens, New York.

A mallet signed by all of my colleagues presented to me when I left the bench. All but one has passed on.

Catching up on work in my study at home. Note the photo of LBJ and me in the background.

In my chambers, searching out research material.

Article featured in the New York Daily News citing my application of, "Christmas Justice."

Christmas Spirit—Joy and Sorrow

Justice Is Dealt, & It Suits Season

By GERALD KESSLER and ARTHUR MULLIGAN

Queens Civil Court Judge Leonard L. Finz invoked what he termed "Christmas justice" yesterday in refusing a mother's request to evict her daughter, son-in-law and their two small children from their house and wants to sell it.

"Two days before Christmas one must reflect upon what is the true meaning of the holiday," Finz said. "Justice is an everyday process but there is also such a thing as Christmas justice.

Pops a Cop & Caps Plea

Lockport, N.Y., Dec. 23 (AP) — Gerald Wagner, 36, of nearby Newfane must tip his hat to every policeman he meets for the next three years.

Judge John V. Hogan of Niagara County Court ordered the fast-tipping Wagner on probation for three years for assaulting a state trooper. He also was fined $300.

Wagner pleaded guilty to resisting arrest. A state policeman said Wagner attacked him when the officer tried to break up a fight between Wagner and his brother.

Christmas is a special holiday which holds a special meaning for millions of people, a day with the family, parents, grandparents and grandchildren.

"I cannot do it."

He Vacates Order

The Judge vacated an eviction warrant obtained by the mother, Mrs. Renee Guillemot of Fort Lauderdale, and ordered a trial for Jan. 8. The action had been brought against Mrs. Guillemot's daughter's husband, Thomas Abbate, also 21, and their children, Thomas Jr., 3, and Jennifer, 2.

Mrs. Guillemot and her husband moved to Florida nearly two years ago and rented the two-family house at 88-16 172d St., Jamaica, to the Abbate family and another. The other family moved out three days ago and a prospective buyer has indicated that he desires to use the entire house for himself, the court was told.

At first the Abbates paid only a nominal $50 a month, but Mrs.

Guillemot raised the rent to $85 a month last summer and then to $175. Abbate, an assistant carpenter, takes home $103 a week and the couple could not pay the higher rent.

In November, the Abbates were served with court papers directing them to pay the rent or get out. They ignored the directive and thus lost any legal standing by default—until they met with Judge Finz yesterday.

When Mrs. Guillemot asked for an immediate trial judge said:

"There is a little ship between mother — you can wait will go home won science tonight family has a ro

Anne Abbate holds daughter, Jennifer, 2, while hubby, Thomas, holds son Thomas Jr., Court, Queens, yesterday after judge invoked "Christmas Justice" in their fam

A Blissful Life Sentence

Putting aside arraignments, pleadings, writs and wrongs for the moment, Judge Leonard Finz of Queens Criminal Court yesterday sentenced a willing young couple to love, honor and obedience 'til death does them part.

The couple were Paul Bloom, 29, an assistant manager of a Washington shoe store, and Susan Katz, 24, of 140-50 Ash Ave., Flushing, Queens. Bloom explained that they'd planned the holiday weekend marriage a long time ago—but finding an available judge was murder.

After a four weeks' search the couple located Judge Finz who scheduled the nuptials—his third of the weekend—for shortly before noon in his chambers.

Susan, radiant in a white lace miniwedding gown, sighed before the ceremony: "I feel kind of numb, I guess it's pretty strange getting married in Criminal Court."

Published in Newsday.

I am in my chambers. 1973.

The large gavel was presented to me by the Brandeis Association as its "Founder," "Chairman of the Board for six years," and "Inspiration." I was also elected, "Lifetime Honorary Chairman of the Board."

JUDGE
LEONARD L. FINZ

MY RESIGNATION AS A NEW YORK STATE
SUPREME COURT JUSTICE

The one major downside to my having become a Civil Court Judge, and later a Supreme Court Justice of New York State, was that these great honors came too early in my career. The result was that I never had the opportunity to earn enough or the wherewithal to comfortably provide for a growing family, college tuitions, and all.

One day, in the early part of 1978, a former professor who taught a post- graduate course I had taken, titled, "Advanced Trial Techniques", prior to my becoming a judge, visited me in chambers. He said he had heard rumors that I was restless and might be interested in using whatever talents I had, not as a judge, but as a trial lawyer. His name was Alfred Julien, a former president of the American Trial Lawyers of America, and in my book, one of the great trial lawyers of the nation, with a reputation to match. He looked me square in the eye and said, "Judge, you were one of my best students. In fact, you were extremely creative, quick on your feet, and showed extraordinary street smarts." It was nice to hear such unsolicited

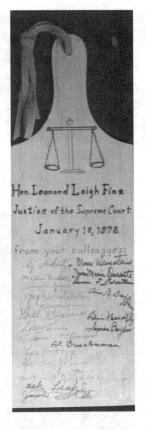

testimonials, but with all humility was hard to believe. What he followed-up with almost knocked me out of my chair. "Quit the bench and join me as a partner in my plaintiff's personal injury firm."

I was suddenly faced with an enormous dilemma. Do I resign my judgeship? On the "No" side of the equation was the advice of my colleagues and prominent lawyers of the county who had an opposite view. They felt that the reputation I had built as a judge would undoubtedly result in my being appointed to the Appellate Court. Some even thought that based upon my judicial standing and the hundreds of written opinions that were heralded and published in the official law books of New York State, I could even be appointed to the State's highest court. But taking the "No" road would still leave me with an uncertain financial future and with a doubtful quality of life that I could provide for my family.

Conversely, a "Yes" decision would immediately remove a very tight financial situation and would evaporate the monetary pressures that weighed so heavily upon me. But despite its short-term positives, it would pose a great risk for me and my family's future security. What if I failed as a trial lawyer? Where would I be then? These were just some of the difficult questions that plagued me.

There were other factors I had to weigh on both sides of the scale. It was not an easy decision to make but after deep thought and long discussions with Pearl, I reached it.

THE DEAL IS SEALED

Within days, and after some hard negotiations, we entered into a contract with a guaranteed income that made my judge's salary pale by comparison. In addition to the elevated financial salary, his firm leased a new Cadillac Elegant to replace the 11-year-old car I had been driving. In addition, the firm agreed also to provide me with a driver, and an assistant to carry-out the leg work on the cases Mr. Julien wanted me to try. The sum of all of its parts is that I was made an offer that would unquestionably change the quality of my family's life. It was an offer (giving full attribution to Mario Puzzo) I could not refuse.

Within a week, I held a press conference to announce my resignation as a Supreme Court Justice of the State of New York, and the financial reasons underscoring my decision. I held it at the New York County Lawyers Association in lower Manhattan. All of the New York City press attended since it was a rarity for a State Supreme Court Justice to leave such a prestigious position. In fact, this was the first such resignation in the memory of many of the press who covered the event. My resignation was of a high judicial position—Supreme Court Justice—a judicial post that most lawyers at the time would have given their right arm to have.

Although I was about to enter a new and exciting career, it still was not the greatest day of my life.

MY FIRST TRIAL

The first case Mr. Julien assigned to me was a personal injury one, to be tried in the Kings County (Brooklyn) Supreme Court. I didn't have a driver as yet, and I drove to the court house. No longer a Supreme Court Justice with special parking privileges, I had to find a parking garage. The closest one was four blocks away. To my  further chagrin, it was one of the coldest days of the winter. I had to carry two heavy litigation bags containing the files I would require for the trial, and carry them with me to the lobby of the courthouse.

Less than a week before when I was still a Supreme Court Justice, I would normally be met by a court officer in the judges' special parking lot, who would then carry whatever I had. Together, we would enter the building through a private entrance, and take a special judge's elevator to my floor.

My new experience in the Brooklyn courthouse where I was no longer a judge, was quite different. Suddenly, I was in the middle of a crowd of people being pushed into an elevator with them. For almost 13 years, I was treated with great respect and reverence as a judge. I was now being shoved around like a soccer ball. It was a trauma to which I was unaccustomed, finding it extremely difficult to deal with at the time. But, it got worse.

When the elevator reached my floor, I proceeded to the assigned courtroom. Waiting for me, was the lawyer who represented the insurance company. He was a well-known fixture in the Brooklyn Supreme Court and had the reputation of being a nasty and aggressive street fighter. He knew who I was and that I had resigned from the Supreme Court just a few days before. As I approached him to say, "Good morning," and to extend my hand as a professional courtesy, his response almost knocked me over. "F**k you. You're nothing but a piece of s**t. You're no longer a f**ken judge, you p***k." I had never been spoken to in such a manner before. For 13 years, I was treated with the utmost courtesy, the same way I treated the hundreds of lawyers and litigants who appeared before me.

My adversary was playing tricks with my head and trying to psyche me out. He was succeeding.

Throughout the trial, he was obnoxiously abusive every time we would pass each other in the hallway. His diatribe and insults never stopped. Did it have an effect upon me? You bet it did. In fact, in the courtroom trial itself and before a jury, I didn't know whether I was a judge or a lawyer. I had such poor grounding that when I would say "objection" to a question posed to a witness by my abusive opponent, I would instinctively rule "sustained," as if I were the judge. After many years of making thousands of rulings as a judge, I was totally thrown by my completely different posture as a lawyer. It was most agonizing and pathetically laughable.

This mayhem went on for more than two weeks. The trial was so hostile, which the jury easily detected to their annoyance. In desperation, I moved for a mistrial. Without hesitation, the trial judge granted it, recognizing that the record could easily support his decision. In addition, I could tell he had enough of the circus and wanted to get out of the case anyway.

MY EMOTIONAL TRAUMA AND ITS AFTERMATH

At the end, I was devastated. It was a disastrous first experience that raised terrible doubts in my head. In fact, the following Sunday, Pearl and I drove out to Jones Beach on Long Island. It was in the height of winter without a single car in the parking lot. I parked and we sat there facing the Atlantic and spoke for two hours. "Did I do the right thing by resigning from the Supreme Court?" I raised the frightening doubts that I perhaps made a colossal mistake in leaving the bench. How in my right mind could I have traded security and respect in exchange for failure and abuse? Pearl listened, and listened, and in her special, bright, and loving way, kept reassuring me that all would work out. She provided hope and confidence. "Sweetheart, this is a difficult adjustment," she said. "You'll find your role. You've got the talent and you'll make a great trial lawyer. All you need is a little more time for the transition. You'll make it. I promise, you'll make it."

I heard those comforting words from Pearl, my wife, my best friend, and ultimately, as was often the case, she was right. Within a month I started to rearrange my head and to gain my footing in the courtroom. My role as judge receded rapidly, as my role as trial lawyer started to rise, steadily. Using a baseball analogy, I was beginning to feel more confident in the batter's box, was able to swing the bat, and might even hit it out of the park. But more about that, later.

After my Brooklyn debacle, I had a number of trials in various courts, each case being satisfactorily settled at different stages of the trial. And with each experience, Pearl's advice was getting closer and closer to the target. I was beginning to adjust to my new role, and could just feel that the home run swing was within my reach.

But even the positive transition to trial lawyer although most welcome, did not make it one of the greatest days of my life.

MY UPSTATE NEW YORK CHALLENGE

I was handed a huge file on a Friday and told that I would have to appear in the Supreme Court in Schenectady, New York, to try the case. I took a quick look at the file. In essence, it claimed that the plaintiff, an elderly woman, developed hives, went to the ER at St. Clare's Hospital, was admitted and treated with Depo-Medrol IV, a cortisone. Several hours later, while still in the hospital room, she suffered a catastrophic stroke which left her with significant defects.

The claim, based upon medical malpractice, was that Depo-Medrol caused the stroke. The difficulty for me was that no medical expert had been engaged by the Julien office to testify, no depositions were ever held, and there was no theory of liability established. I was faced with a gigantic problem and had little time to resolve it. Reading portions of the file, I observed that the case had been adjourned so many times through the years that the Schenectady judge had set it down "final" for Monday or it would be dismissed. This was quite a challenge.

Another major difficulty was that when the retainer was signed years before, Julien, at the client's insistence, committed that only he and no other lawyer in his firm would try the case. That was an absolute condition stressed by the client who said he would not accept anyone else other than Julien himself. That is, until the client was told that a former New York State Supreme Court Justice would be the lawyer assigned to represent his wife at trial. The "Judge" in front of my name was most persuasive in getting the husband to finally agree to the change.

Advising other clients (who similarly would only settle for Julien, and no other attorney to try their case), that a former high-ranking Judge was now his partner and would personally be their trial attorney, received consent in every case. This was probably one of the reasons Julien met my contract demands as a further inducement for me to leave the bench and to become his partner.

I spent the next hours reading medical articles and textbooks so that I could familiarize myself with the anatomy involved and the causal link between Depo-Medrol and stroke, if any. After reading all the articles I could find, and after intensive research, I came up with a theory that to me at least appeared somewhat plausible. But I now needed a qualified medical expert to support it. I called at least five practicing neurologists in the city. None of them would agree to testify. Time was running out and I had to find a medical expert who would be willing to testify on this most difficult case.

Having been rejected by the medical doctors I called as possible experts, my only alternative was to try to reach out to a retired neurologist in Florida.

MY MEET WITH A MEDICAL EXPERT

After many phone calls, I finally located a doctor who appeared slightly interested. To further his interest, I told him I would arrange first class air travel from Florida to Schenectady, New York, that all incidental expenses would be paid, and that he would of course be paid additionally for his time. To assure his willingness to testify, I told him he

could bring his wife along whose expenses would similarly be paid. I even said I would provide Broadway show tickets should they decide to spend any time in New York City.

Following my proposal, and after hearing the theory of liability I developed against the hospital based upon the medical journals and texts, he finally agreed that with a reasonable degree of medical certainty, the theory I laid out sounded medically plausible. That accomplished, I arranged to meet with him on Sunday morning at a specific hotel in Schenectady to review the entire case.

I spent most of the day with him on Sunday, and when we had completed our in-depth discussions, I at least had an expert who would testify on behalf of the plaintiff stroke victim. The next day being Monday, my assigned young assistant, a lawyer for only two months, and I, reported to the trial judge's chambers. When I entered the room, there were several court officers, a stenographic reporter, the attorney who represented the defendant hospital, several of his assistants, and the trial judge who was sitting behind a large desk. I knew that the judge and defense lawyer knew each other well, as is usually the case in upstate smaller communities. But that was a situation I would just have to deal with in a professional way during the trial.

The first words out of the defense lawyer's mouth were, "Did you drive all the way from the city of New York for this piece of crap?" I ignored the put-down. My skin was already quite thickened through my steady adjustment and ignored his obvious attempt to do head tricks on me. Looking straight at the judge, I said in a most humble and respectful tone, "Good Morning, Your Honor. My name is Leonard Finz (he knew who I was) and I represent the plaintiff. I am here ready to try this case." "Okay," the judge replied. "See you in the courtroom. Bailiff, bring up a jury panel."

THE VERDICT

The trial lasted more than three weeks. When concluded, the jury deliberated for six hours and returned a verdict for my client in the sum of one million five hundred thousand dollars. When it was all over, the defense lawyer (the same guy

who greeted me with "Did you drive all the way from the city of New York for this crap?"), a big 6'3" stiff who always wore a bow tie approached me and said, "So tell me Len, is this the largest medical malpractice verdict you ever got?" My response to him intending to shoot him right between the eyes was, "Well to tell you the truth, this is the first medical malpractice case I ever tried." With that, his 6'3" frame shrunk closer to my 5'8" size. The case was written up by the *New York Times* as having achieved the highest medical malpractice verdict in New York State (this was 1978, almost 40 years ago). Newsday also wrote it up with a feature story and a headline, "Former Judge Triumphs as Lawyer".

But even that great win with all of its accolades, did not bring about the greatest day of my life.

A LANDMARK DES VAGINAL CANCER CASE

In the spring of 1978, after trying case after case successfully, I returned to my office after having received a large verdict following a three-week trial. When I entered the room, I was shocked to see large red folders lined up on the floor around the perimeter of the office. It seemed as if my office had been turned into a file room. When I asked what, those files were doing there, I was told they all contained massive documents in a DES case which was the next one I was scheduled to try. "DES?" I asked, "What is DES?" I was then told that DES stood for "Diethylstilbestrol", a drug that had been given to pregnant woman during the 1940's and 1950's. It had been developed as a pharmaceutical product to be prescribed to those women who had a history of miscarriages. It was promoted as a miracle drug that would permit the pregnancy to proceed to full term.

Later, it was discovered through medical articles that appeared in prestigious journals, that in a certain percentage of births, females who reached their late teenage years developed clear cell carcinoma of the vagina. These articles raised the possibility that the DES pills ingested by the pregnant mother when the teenage girls were in utero, was the causative link to the vaginal cancer they developed years after their birth.

Many cases were brought against DES manufacturers throughout the country, all of which resulted in verdicts in favor of the pharmaceutical companies. With that as a backdrop, I was now faced with having to try a DES case on behalf of Joyce Bichler, a young lady who had been diagnosed with vaginal cancer at age 18, and the daughter of a mother who had taken DES during her pregnancy. The central issues for me at the time were almost insurmountable since there were more than three hundred manufacturers of DES during the period in which Joyce's mother had ingested DES pills. Under the law that applied in New York (and most other states), in order to hold a manufacturer liable, it had to be proven that the specific DES taken by the mother was the actual product of the manufacturer named as a defendant. With the passage of nineteen years and the loss and destruction of medical records, this was a legal burden that was almost impossible to overcome.

Consequently, and strategically, the suit had been brought against the largest manufacturer of DES, Eli Lilly & Co., on the theory that it was the largest manufacturer of the drug and its only aggressive marketer. That DES would never have seen the light of day and would never have been manufactured by any other drug maker had Lilly not have been the major promoter of it. Since we could not prove that the DES taken by Joyce's mother was a Lilly pill, I argued that Lilly was just as liable to Joyce as if Lilly had been the actual manufacturer of the pills taken by her mother many years before.

The lawyers who represented Lilly had a highly trained team that had defended many DES cases successfully. The unit was led by Russell "Cap" Beatty, a top litigator with the major Wall Street law firm of Dewey, Ballentine, Palmer, Bushby, and Wood. Within one week, I put together whatever experts I could find who would support the theory I was pressing. Days later, we proceeded to a trial in the New York State Supreme Court before an extremely strict judge, Arnold Fraiman, who prior to becoming a New York State Supreme Court Justice had been the Commissioner of Investigation, having been appointed by Mayor John Lindsay.

What follows is taken *verbatim* from a book titled, "DES Daughter", authored by Joyce Bichler, my client, and published by Avon Books, a division of the Hearst Corporation.

"The closing arguments were very important. This trial had gone on for so many weeks, and so much highly technical information had been presented to the jury, that it was important to summarize the major points, bring them all together again to refresh the jurors' memories."

"Mr. Beatie was first to present his argument..."

MY TURN TO SUM UP TO THE JURY

"Now it was Judge Finz's moment. He stood up and his force seemed to fill the room. He was fighting to the end. He began by emphasizing that in the 1940s DES was known to have the potential to cause harm to the fetus, yet it was never properly tested before being prescribed to pregnant women. He reiterated the point that by 1953, DES was known not to be effective in preventing miscarriage, yet it was left on the market. He repeated that DES had caused my cancer, that had the DES not acted as a trigger, I would not have developed this cancer. Judge Finz sounded quite lyrical as he used the analogy of rising steam. When someone draws up a bathtub full of steaming hot water, he said, if they are prudent they do not just jump into the tub without first testing the water with a finger or toe to see how hot it is. In the 1940s, Finz continued, the information on DES showed that the drug, like steaming hot water, had the potential for causing great harm. A prudent pharmaceutical company should have seen the steam rising and done proper animal tests before giving DES to pregnant women, thereby plunging them into the steaming bathwater, where they were scalded. The analogy was brilliant.

"Judge Finz went on. He emphasized the significance of the drug companies having acted in concert to get DES approved and explained again why we were holding Eli Lilly & Co. responsible as the leading manufacturer of the drug. Then, as he talked again about my injuries, I remembered his eulogy on Truth. He did not dramatize or over emphasize anything. He simply described what had happened to me in the tone of honesty and genuine sympathy that left my eyes and many others' teary. It was the perfect approach.

"Finz spoke for several hours. He built up to a crescendo of emotion. He was filled with feeling as he stood in front of the jury and said..."

PART OF MY SUMMATION

"We are outraged at the tragedy of being victimized and used as (the pharmaceutical company's) human guinea pigs. Let us demand that the drugs being sold and put into the market for profit are effective and safe for human use.

"We cannot here alter the course of injustice that can be found right here even in the Bronx County. But we can here alter the course of this major injustice that has been perpetrated by this giant drug industry and be heard through the greatest power that we will still here have in our democratic society, your voice as a juror.

"Few people, ladies and gentlemen, will ever be given the rare opportunity that you have in this case as independent and enlightened citizens. Few people in this world will ever have the opportunity that belongs to you today, that opportunity to say in this courtroom for everyone to hear, 'We are outraged at being used. We are outraged at being manipulated for profit. We are outraged at having been victimized and neglected with a lack of concern. We are people. We are human. Our lives are precious to us. Our lives count. Our health rights must be protected, and we are not going to permit this outrage to continue.'

"A little over a hundred years ago, a great president stood in a stilled battlefield on Pennsylvania soil and said, 'The world will little note nor long remember what we say here but can never forget what they did here.'

"This courtroom, ladies and gentlemen, is a battlefield. And this battle is one that truly pits the individual against the mighty. And let the women and men and children of our country, whose lives will surely be affected by the decision you will reach today, know that when history records your deeds it was done here by six proud, independent, courageous people in the Bronx. And let this be the step that links each of you with the progress of the future.

"We cannot expect to reach all of our goals and remove all injustice today. But today let us take the first step. Today, let us have courage. Today, let us demand that the standards be held high. Let us demand that those who commit wrongs upon us and our children and our children's children must be held accountable so that tomorrow and the tomorrows that come, there will be a world where safer drugs will be provided for our children and our

children's children, free of the tragic consequences of careless acts and full of the assurance that the Joyce Bichler tragedy must never, never happen again in this nation."

"By the time he had finished, he looked exhausted but satisfied. I could hardly contain my gratitude to him; he had outdone himself..."

THE DES VERDICT AND ITS AFTERMATH

After nine weeks of trial, and six days of deliberations, the jury returned a verdict on behalf of Joyce Bichler against Eli Lilly & Co. It was the only DES verdict ever won in the country at the time against any pharmaceutical manufacturer. Lilly filed an appeal and lost. Lilly filed the next appeal to the highest court of the State of New York, and lost. Lilly, however, did not stop there. It appealed to the United States Supreme Court, was summarily denied, and "Joyce Bichler vs Eli Lilly & Co.", became the law of the land. By way of its impact on justice, it opened the courthouse doors for thousands of DES victims, who up until the Bichler case, were for the most part, denied entrance. The Bichler result and its underlying rationale are included in the syllabus of almost every law school in the nation.

As to its further impact in New York State, my son Stuart Finz, an outstanding trial lawyer (he received the only verdict in New York against Phillip Morris—the largest cigarette manufacturer in the world—on behalf of a lung cancer victim), became chairman of the statewide official DES committee overseeing the ways and means in which further victims could be protected from the irresponsible conduct of DES manufacturers.

But even the great kudos I received from DES daughters and the public at large, although most appreciated, did not produce the greatest day of my life.

A DEFENDANT NEUROSURGEON
BLURTS OUT INSTINCTIVELY

I represented a woman (the plaintiff) who claimed that following a subdural injection given by a neurosurgeon (the defendant) to relieve back pain, she suffered permanent residual headaches. The trial was held in another state before a jury.

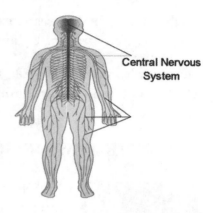

Central Nervous System

I called the defendant neurosurgeon as my first witness. Using a 30x40 blank board placed on a tripod, I asked questions to establish the detailed human anatomy of the brain at the top, ultimately concluding with the *cauda equine* at the bottom.

With each step, I would proceed to the next part of the anatomy that involved the entire central nervous system. As he was affirming each question addressed to the anatomy, I would draw that anatomical part on the 30x40 board using large colorful markers. Although the jury could not see what I was doing with the board (since it was not in evidence), I kept my "art work" out of their and the witness's view, exposing only the blank reverse side of the board sitting on the tripod.

Having received the appropriate answers in support of my anatomical drawing, I then carried the 30x40 board (still out of the view of the jury who by this time had leaned forward, giving rapt attention to what I was doing, wondering what was contained on the board) to the neurosurgeon on the witness stand.

Showing the witness what I had drawn based upon his responses to my questions, I then asked, "Doctor___, I show you this drawing and ask if that is a fair and reasonable representation of the central nervous system you just described?" Shocked, he answered, "Yes." With this courtroom procedure, my credibility with the jury rose one thousand percent.

Having answered, "Yes," I could then offer it and have it marked in evidence. Once done, the jury, already riveted to the whole process, was now permitted under the rules to review my drawing. The neurosurgeon displayed a mixture of shock and admiration, instinctively blurting out, "How do you know so much about the anatomy of the central nervous system?" To which (while turning to face the jury), I casually replied, "Doctor_____, the ability to read the English language is not the exclusive province of the medical profession." The jury and judge let out a howling laugh, and with that response I was on my way to establishing the high credibility and strategy I planned.

Incidentally, when the trial was completed, the jury returned a verdict which was the highest recorded in that state at the time.

THE LAW OFFICES OF LEONARD L. FINZ

In 1984, six years after joining the Julien firm, and after scoring record verdicts from Brooklyn to Buffalo, New York, and in other states, I decided to start my own firm so that my son Stuart and son-in-law Jerry Parker, both lawyers, could one day partner-up with me. The firm was located at 217 Broadway, just one block from the World Trade Center. After five years and requiring more space, we moved across the street to the Swiss Bank Building located at 222 Broadway. The name of the firm was changed to Finz and Finz some years later. When I reached the age of 80, I retired from the active practice of law, my son Stuart Finz, becoming CEO of the firm.

He has since achieved remarkable success as one of the premier trial lawyers in New York State. My son-in law, Jerry Parker, has his own firm, Parker and Waichman LLP, and has developed a huge national reputation as a mass tort attorney, involved mostly with multiple district litigation. Both Stuart and Jerry have scored the highest marks amongst their peers.

As for me, some years ago I was peer-reviewed and designated as one of the "Preeminent trial lawyers of America", the highest and most coveted rating as published by Martindale-Hubble (the most respected and authoritative lawyers' directory in the nation).

THE SYSTEMATIC EXCLUSION OF
BLACKS FROM A JURY

In 1986, the United State Supreme Court in Batson v Kentucky held that a prosecutor in a criminal trial could not systematically exclude blacks from a jury. In that criminal case, the defendant was black. Black jurors who were called to the box were all challenged by the prosecutor who used his peremptory challenges (a limited number is allotted to each side and can be used for any reason) to remove black jurors from serving on the jury.

The defendant was found guilty by an all-white jury, with an appeal going all the way to the Supreme Court of the United States. The court reversed the conviction and sent the case back for a new trial, holding that the systematic striking of black jurors in a criminal trial without a valid reason for doing so, violated the Constitution of the United States.

MY FIGHT FOR THE RIGHTS OF BLACK JURORS

Now, to my case...

The year was 1987. I represented a black woman who had slipped on ice at the entrance of a Manhattan office building. I claimed that a defect caused water to drip onto the entrance walk which later froze into ice creating a

dangerous condition that caused her to fall, fracturing her leg. The defense vigorously disagreed, and thus the trial...

At jury selection, two black jurors' names were picked randomly out of the jury drum. They took seats on the proposed jury. When it came time for challenges, the defendant's attorney used two of his three peremptory challenges to strike the black jurors from the jury. At the end, I was left with a totally white jury. Without delay, I advised the defense attorney that I wanted to see the judge (no judge had presided at jury selection). Together with defendant's counsel, we appeared before a judge, at which time I made a motion to disband the jury, citing *Batson v Kentucky*, the United States

Supreme Court decision as authority. My adversary was quick to argue that the *Batson* case applied only to a criminal trial and not to a civil case.

The judge listened intently as I argued there was no substantial difference as to whether the case was a criminal or civil one. If indeed, the two black jurors were systematically excused because of their color (in the absence of any valid reason), the holding in the *Batson* case should be just as relevant in a civil case. With the request that we remain in the courtroom, the judge exited and entered his chambers. Within fifteen minutes he returned and rendered his decision. He granted my motion, ordered that the present jury be disbanded and that a new panel be drawn.

It was the first time in New York State history, and possibly the nation, that a systematic exclusion of black jurors in a <u>civil</u> case was held to be a violation of the equal protection clause of the Fourteenth Amendment of the Constitution of the United States.

With a new jury drawn, two of the six jurors were black. After a two-week trial, a verdict was returned for my client in the sum of $1.7 million, the highest in New York State for that kind of injury at the time (more than thirty years ago). The case, because of its novelty, received a major front page story in the *New York Law Journal* and other media.

Even making such new and just law, did not rise to being the greatest day of my life.

MY ROLE IN A FAVORITE SOAP OPERA CALLED "ANOTHER WORLD"

Sometime in the late 1990's and during the time I ran my own firm in downtown Manhattan, I received a phone call from an NBC TV executive who asked if I would be willing to act the role of a judge in their popular and long running soap opera, "Another World". The producer had heard and seen me on the Larry King and other talk shows and thought I would be perfect for the part. He informed me also, that it would involve at least a full month of my time. Given my show biz roots, my answer was an obvious one. I was not TV shy, having appeared on almost every talk show in New York including *The Today Show* with Katie Couric, Larry King, Joan Rivers, Bill O'Reilly, Dan Rather, Phil Donohue, ABC's *20/20* with Dianne Sawyer, and more. I was also featured on a TV network show with Roy Cohen, the former counsel to the infamous Senator Joe McCarthy. Acting in front of the camera, I thought, would be an exciting treat that would take me back to my early entertainment days. For one month, I appeared on every segment presiding at a murder trial in which one of the protagonists was being accused of homicide. Of course, I was the butt of some jokes from some of my friends and colleagues, but all was done with good humor.

Although I found the soap opera to be filled with a different kind of fun and excitement (being surrounded by producers, directors, cameras, actors, and sponsors), the sum total of it all did not rise to being the greatest day of my life.

MY SAD VISIT TO 9/11 AND GROUND ZERO

Throughout our lives, there are events so shocking that they always seem to invite the same questions. "Where were you on Pearl Harbor Day?" "Where were you when President Kennedy was assassinated?" "Where were you on 9/11?"

Those of us old enough to have lived through those tragedies will be able to provide the most detailed answer to those questions. Although I was around for all three devastating events, I'll discuss only 9/11...

It was September 11, 2001, as I was leaving my home heading for the federal courthouse at Foley Square in lower Manhattan, when my wife called out to me, anxiously reporting that an airplane had just struck one of the towers of the World Trade Center. What happened after that event is unfortunately dark history and requires no further discussion regarding its horror.

What is a touch of irony, however, is that prior to 9/11, our law firm occupied the entire top 27th floor of the Swiss Bank Building located at

222 Broadway. My corner office had large picture windows that faced the twin towers of the World Trade Center just one block to the west. It was a majestic view. But our ten-year lease was about to expire and we were looking for space more suited to our growing needs. A few weeks before 9/11, we were in continuing negotiations, seriously considering to lease space on the 84th floor of the North Tower. Somehow, we made a last-minute decision to move our firm elsewhere. Call it fate.

My good friend Milton Mollen, a former Presiding Justice of the Appellate Division, Second Department, and a former New York City Deputy Mayor who was heading up a city commission that bore his name at the time, invited me to join him for a special tour of Ground Zero. This was just days after 9/11. I agreed to join him.

The air was rancid. The smell of smoke and chemicals permeated the eerie atmosphere that surrounded twisted steel girders and massive rubble. The whole area looked like the set of a horror movie. The air was so contaminated we had to wear masks (which I have kept all these years). The sad memory of that enormous ground filled with tragedy and devastation with all of the innocent lives that were lost has never left me.

It was an enormously heartbreaking and extremely emotional experience. Needless to say, it was not one of the greatest days of my life.

THE BATTLE OF TWO GIANTS

Attorney Leonard Finz, Gloria Hall and attorney Michael Kaplen (l. to r.) after record $9 million damages award in Brooklyn Supreme Court yesterday.

Since the beginning of time, powerful forces have fought each other with innocent victims being caught in the middle. As a trial lawyer, I saw first-hand how five thousand years of historical battles had been brought into a modern New York courtroom.

This is the compelling story...

A powerful force known as Con Edison collided with another powerful force, the Samuel Lefrak organization, with my client, the victim in the middle of their private battle.

Lefrak, one of the largest developers of high rise buildings in New York City, operated the one in which my client was a tenant. Unbeknown to her or the hundreds of her tenant neighbors, there had been an ongoing dispute between Con Ed and Lefrak regarding utility bills that Con Ed claimed were owed by Lefrak. Conversely, Lefrak argued it was Con Ed that in fact owed huge refunds to Lefrak for overcharges. The building in which my client had an apartment on the twelfth floor was the subject of dispute.

Failing to pay the building's bills for six months chargeable to Lefrak, Con Ed sent a team of men surreptitiously dressed as elevator repairmen into the building on a Friday night. Secretly, they made their way into the power room, disconnected all electric lines, leaving the high rise building in total darkness.

With no choice, the tenants had to walk up or down the staircases with flashlights or candles just to get to their apartments or out to the street.

My client was a certified nurse assistant who at the time was caring for a patient living three floors below. Knowing that her patient needed assistance, particularly in the dark, my client entered the pitch-black stairway, and with flashlight in hand started to walk down the three flights. Due to the darkness, she missed a step, fell down a number of stairs and suffered a serious back injury.

The case could not be settled since each powerhouse defendant pointed to the other as the one responsible. They thought only of their own self-interests, and cared little about the victims who would be caught in the middle of their battle (human nature hadn't changed in five thousand years).

With neither defendant yielding, I tried the case to its conclusion. The jury deliberated for less than two hours. When they re-entered the courtroom, the foreman, (a self-employed carpenter who probably earned no more than three hundred dollars a week in those days), got up, stood tall, looked around the courtroom and announced the verdict. "We the jury find for the plaintiff against both defendants in the sum of," he hesitated, let out a whimsical smile in our direction, and continued, "we find for the plaintiff... in the sum of nine million dollars."

Although the history of two Goliaths hadn't changed, justice was at least done by the verdict, it being the largest one of its kind at the time. The record result and what led up to it became a major story with photos of me, my client, and assistant, on the front pages of the New York press.

But despite our celebration and the elation of my client (the innocent victim who found herself in the middle of the battle between two powerful forces), it still did not rise to being the greatest day of my life.

TRAGEDY AND JOY

When I was a Judge, many of my colleagues were reluctant to perform marriage ceremonies for personal or other reasons. As such, the clerk of the court would usually call me when a couple needed a judge to perform their nuptials. I would never say no, and I would perform their wedding in chambers during my lunch hour since I didn't want to inconvenience litigants and lawyers before me by having them wait while I engaged in a wedding ritual. All of this takes me to a tragic and joyful story...

A recognized charity was holding a bike-a-thon in the late 1980's to raise money for its cause. With the guidance of New York State, a two-lane state highway that ran adjacent to Jones Beach, Long Island, was selected where hundreds of cyclists would ride together over a designated route that covered about ten miles. For that purpose, the two-lane road, one going east, the other west, was shut down to auto traffic, to be used solely for the bike-a-thon. The composition of the roads was concrete, separated by a tar-filled expansion joint.

My client (I'll call him "Richard") was among the hundreds of cyclists participating in the event. In his 50's, married with two grown children, he started to ride with others in the large group when the front tire of his bicycle suddenly got stuck in a narrow expansion joint bringing his bike to a sudden halt, propelling him airborne and striking the concrete road with such violent impact as to render him a quadriplegic.

We at Finz & Finz brought suit against New York State since its agents had approved the state road to be used for the bike-a-thon despite its potential danger of expansion-joint narrowing which posed a hazard. I settled the suit in the New York Court of Claims for five million dollars plus a waiver of hundreds of thousands owed for medical and hospital bills. The millions that Richard and his family received at least provided financial security for life. They were extremely grateful for having achieved the settlement, which also set a record in the Court of Claims at that time.

About one year later, I received a call from Richard's wife who told me their daughter was getting married, that she had sent a letter to an organization explaining her father's most unfortunate situation and that she and her future husband could not afford a honeymoon. This news reached the Ringling Brothers Barnum and Bailey Circus scheduled to begin a two-week run at the Nassau Veterans Memorial Coliseum in Uniondale, New York. Upon hearing their difficult plight, they offered to provide a luxurious honeymoon with all expenses paid, gifts, and cash, if they would hold their wedding on Saturday, the opening night of the circus to be held at the Coliseum. They were told that the circus performance would be halted for 15 minutes, at which time the wedding ceremony would be held in the center ring before thousands in the audience.

For them, the Barnum and Bailey offer was a fabulous dream come true, everything that any young couple could ever wish for but they needed a judge to perform the wedding. Thus, the call to me.

Although I was no longer a judge, I still by law had the right to perform a wedding ceremony in New York State. My answer of course was, "I'd be so honored to do it."

A THREE RING WEDDING

When Saturday evening arrived, I drove to the Coliseum, parked my car, and was escorted to a holding area within the huge arena. The circus was in progress, full of its typical sounds and spirited brassy music. There, seated in a flower-decked chariot with two white horses were Richard's daughter and her husband-to-be both outfitted beautifully, she in a stunning white wedding gown, he in a handsome white tuxedo.

I put on my black judicial robe and took a seat opposite them. Within moments, all the loud action of the circus came to a halt as the ring announcer shouted out, "And here they come—the bride and groom."

The big colorful band played the wedding march as the horse drawn chariot made its way to the center ring amidst all of the spectacular spot lights and fanfare.

I performed the wedding ceremony within fifteen minutes and when I said, "I now pronounce you man and wife," the thousands in the packed arena went wild as balloons and confetti dropped from above while the large brass band played a Sousa march. After the ceremony, I walked over to Richard seated in his wheelchair, congratulated him and his wife, hugged the two of them for at least ten seconds or more as tears continued to flow down Richard's cheeks.

I left shortly thereafter and drove home. When I arrived, Pearl told me she had seen it all on Channel 12, the local news station. We hugged and I could feel her tears since she knew of the terrible accident that made Richard a quadriplegic victim. I had terribly mixed feelings that night—saddened by the horrendous tragedy Richard and his family were living through but also contrasted by some measure of joy I had brought to such dear people who even for that short period in their terribly troubled lives could replace their long suffering with such heartfelt happiness.

THE PROVERB TEST... OOPS

One of the issues in a trial in which a young man (my client), who was struck by a train, was whether in addition to other significant injuries, he suffered Post-Traumatic Stress Disorder (PTSD). The trial was held in the federal court of another state presided over by a very strict and rigid judge.

In defense of the PTSD claim, the railroad attorney produced a psychiatrist as a witness. He testified that he had examined the young plaintiff at the request of the railroad and in addition to other tests that he, the psychiatrist had created, he gave my client the "proverb" test. In his explanation of it, the witness stated he would quote a proverb and based upon the meaning given to it, he could then draw certain conclusions as to whether the young plaintiff was indeed suffering from PTSD, or faking it.

The psychiatrist testified he quoted three separate proverbs, thereafter asking my client for his interpretation. For example, one proverb was, "A rolling stone gathers no moss". He would then ask my client what he thought it meant. Another was, "An apple does not fall far from the tree". Same question to my client regarding his interpretation of that proverb. A third proverb quoted was, "A stitch in time saves nine".

Based upon the responses received, the psychiatrist concluded that my young client did not suffer from PTSD. The sum of his testimony appeared somewhat credible, but as one of the grand masters of evidence once wrote, "Cross-examination is the greatest legal engine to get to the truth."

I began my cross-exam by asking if he had ever published his "proverb" test? (I knew he hadn't since it never came up in any of my prior research.) I then attacked him on having exaggerated several of his credentials regarding the teaching position he claimed to have had with a leading university. For example, he stated he was a professor, when in truth a recent faculty bulletin listed him as an "Instructor". I had some fun with that one. In preparation of the trial, my research team discovered other discrepancies in his background.

He admitted he had reviewed several hundred cases for the defendant through the years and had testified in court on its behalf more than a dozen times (again, I was armed with this information, anyway). He was then asked, what percentage of his total income he received from the railroad? (I knew the answer from prior court transcripts.) He answered he didn't know precisely. I then hit him with, "Well didn't you testify in '*Jones v Railroad*, etc.,' that sixty percent of your income came from the defendant railroad?" He had to answer, "Yes." since I had the transcripts in my hand ready to pounce upon him if he had given me a contradictory answer.

Having established enough of a predicate that the major part of his income came from the very defendant railroad in the case and that just moments ago he concluded my young client did not suffer from PTSD, I then continued, "I was very impressed by your 'proverb' test." He answered, "Thank you." My response was, "Before you thank me, I now have another question for you..."

"You stated that sixty percent of your income comes from the defendant. That being the case, allow me to give you the 'proverb' test of which you are so proud. Would you please face the jury and give your interpretation of this proverb? "Do not bite the hand that feeds you."

The jury and even the hardened federal judge broke out with laughter. As the witness hesitated and started almost hysterically double-talking a ridiculous response, I interrupted, "I have no further questions," and sat down. The damage was done.

Within a few days, we left the federal courthouse with a record settlement.

CHAOS IN THE COURTROOM

Seeing what he believed to be a car going through a stop sign, the NYPD patrol car with siren and flashing lights made chase. The private vehicle stopped and the police officer exited his car. He walked over to the driver's side and was about to ask for a registration and license. But before he could even get his words out, the car took off.

Instinctively, the officer drew his sidearm and fired two rounds at the fleeing car. Both missed, except that the second bullet struck a young woman who was wheeling a baby carriage on the sidewalk one hundred yards away. Tragically, she was declared dead at the scene.

We were retained by the family and brought a civil wrongful death suit against the City of New York, and the police officer. Throughout the pre-trial process, the city pressed the defense that the fleeing driver had used his vehicle as a weapon to run the officer down. As such, the city through its torts department and comptroller, made no attempt to settle the claim, thus requiring a trial.

It was 1982 and as usual it was a case in which Julien had been retained with the condition that he, and only he, would try the matter. But as with other cases that had been in the file room for years, the trial was assigned to me and the family finally consented to having "Judge Finz" try it in place of Julien.

At the trial, a young assistant corporation counsel appeared on behalf of the city and police officer. Within a short time, I could sense he was extremely nervous, seemed to lack much experience, and as humbly as I can put it, I was just too much for him. The truth is that he was assigned to a situation and an adversary that were both way over his head.

Through the many years as a judge combined with my experience as a trial lawyer, I had a strong feeling that the jury was with us all the way and that I was heading toward a huge verdict.

When all of the proof was in on both sides, it was now summation time. Under New York rules, the party that has the burden of proof in a civil case (the plaintiff), has the right to deliver an opening first, and is last to sum- up. That meant the young assistant corporation counsel would deliver his summation before mine.

IT LOOKED LIKE A HEART ATTACK OR STROKE

He faced the jury and started to speak, but within ten minutes, his words became garbled, his face turned sheet-white and stared at the ceiling as he began mumbling incoherently. Witnessing this, I ran up to him in a flash, pulled up a chair and sat him down. Mayhem took over as the judge ordered a court officer to take the jury out of the courtroom. As they were exiting I yelled out in the loudest voice, "Get oxygen in here, now. Call 911."

Stroke – there's treatment if you act FAST.

Face Face look uneven? **A**rm One arm hanging down? **S**peech Slurred speech? **T**ime Call 911 NOW!

1623 New York State Department of Health 4/07

The judge seemed to be stuck in shock, but seeing what was happening in front of him, he quickly came out of it and ordered another court officer in the courtroom to follow what I had just yelled out.

I hurriedly loosened the young man's tie, held both his hands, repeating he should take deep breaths, while assuring him over and over that he would be okay. He just sat there, shaking, staring straight ahead and mumbling to himself.

Within ten minutes, an EMT crew arrived, took vital signs, put an oxygen mass over his face, placed him on a gurney and whisked him out. Responding to my question, one of the EMT techs gave me the name of the ER and hospital he was being taken to. I then asked the judge if I could leave the courtroom for an hour or so since I wanted to proceed directly to the hospital. Permission was granted and I ran out of the courthouse directly to my car, and instructed my driver to rush me to the ER.

I remained at the hospital for over an hour and was relieved to receive word from the ER doctor that the young assistant corporation counsel had only suffered an anxiety attack, and that he was coming around and should be okay within a few hours. It was good news. I then returned to the courthouse.

The judge had already declared a mistrial. After almost three weeks of a completed trial, I would have to start from scratch with a new jury. But seeing how the city's defense was demolished, and the real potential for a huge verdict in a second trial, the chief of the New York City's torts division and I with the judge's assistance, entered into a settlement. It was a record sum. The specific amount, although quite high, cannot be disclosed due to a confidential agreement entered into.

I felt sorry for the young man who never should have been assigned to try such an inflammatory case in addition to everything else.

With all the excitement and chaos (fortunately, an anxiety attack and not a heart attack or stroke), and despite a record settlement reached, it was not the greatest day of my life.

CUP OF JOE COSTS $3 MILLION

An employee was sent out to buy coffee for coworkers. There was a luncheonette four blocks away and rather than walk she decided to drive there with her own car. On the way, she struck my 10-year-old client who sustained serious injuries.

In our preliminary discussions with her lawyer we were told, "Sorry, pal. She's got no insurance. It lapsed when she failed to pay the premium due."

With a sharp pivot, we sued her employer, claiming that at the time of the accident she was on the job. Therefore, I argued to the judge, her negligence in hitting the kid should be chargeable to her employer who did have insurance.

After hearing both sides of the argument, the judge agreed. The case was settled just before jury selection for a whopping $3 million.

There is a back human interest story I must share... Earlier in this memoir I described the first trial I had in Brooklyn, New York, three days after I resigned from the Supreme Court. The lawyer in that case called me every filthy name trying to psych me out by doing head tricks on me. And he succeeded! That was almost ten years earlier when I had such a disastrous experience due to the gutter tactics he employed. It was now my turn for a little bit of retribution.

That Brooklyn street fighter was the same hot shot in this case who now represented the employer, except I was far too seasoned for him to use any of his cruddy shtick on me this time. In fact, he folded up like an accordion knowing I had built an arsenal of courtroom weaponry with all the big wins since my first disgusting encounter with him.

After the settlement was put on the record, I walked out with my happy clients and intentionally strutted past the lawyer as I was leaving the courtroom. I looked straight at him, threw him a smile, and with a satisfying smirk, said, "Now that you've agreed to pay $3 million, I hope you have a nice day," as I walked away trying to restrain a hearty laugh.

THE HELMET THAT FAILED

She was a passenger on a motorcycle sitting behind her fiancé who was operating it, when the bike was struck violently by a car. She went flying through the air and landed on her head. Although wearing a Bell helmet, she suffered brain damage.

We sued the manufacturer of the helmet (the car had only $25,000 of insurance which was thrown in right away), it being the largest manufacturer of helmets in the industry, and the supplier of hundreds of police departments throughout the country. Although sued many times, Bell Helmet Co. never lost a case.

With great effort, I located an expert in the Midwest, a mechanical engineer with good credentials, and had him perform impact tests on the helmet. As suspected, there was a very subtle defect that led to the failure of the helmet to absorb the penetrating G-forces (energy) under certain severe impact conditions.

Although my adversary fought all the way, the jury returned a verdict of $3 million (that was thirty-five years ago). It was the first verdict against Bell, who as a result changed the design of the helmet so as to fully absorb the G-forces that would be violently released in a serious impact situation.

I was real proud of what my efforts brought about. Fighting for the consumer and elevating safety was indeed most gratifying.

But despite it all and the good that it did for the consumer, it still was not the greatest day of my life.

ATTACHING THE LEFT FOOT TO THE RIGHT LEG

Walking through one train car to another on a Conrail train, she fell between the two cars and onto the tracks. The train ran over her legs and severed her left foot and right leg.

A passenger pulled the emergency cord, the train came to a sudden halt, paramedics appeared shortly thereafter and rushed the victim to Belleview Hospital in Manhattan. Her severed limbs were placed in ice bags and rushed to the hospital by police car.

Upon arrival at Belleview, the victim was taken immediately to the OR where a team of micro surgeons operated on her for over eight hours trying to reattach her severed limbs. Her right foot was beyond attachment as was

162

her left leg above the ankle. Working tirelessly, the surgeons performed micro surgery by, "reattaching the severed left foot to her right leg in the first microsurgical lower limb transposition performed in the United States." (As reported by newsman, Bernard Rabin.)

It was miraculous surgery performed by an incredibly talented and dedicated team of micro surgeons.

I settled the case for $5 million against Conrail for having a dangerous space between two connected trains large enough for such a tragedy to occur. It was the highest settlement of its kind at the time. But the biggest story was the unbelievable microsurgery performed by a superb team of surgeons at Belleview who combined skill, creativity, and medical inspiration, to leave the victim with at least one good foot.

What the surgeons accomplished was deserving of the highest award for community service far beyond the call—and probably one of the greatest days of <u>their</u> lives.

CHANGE THE SPOTLIGHT UP THERE

He was a 28-year-old stage hand in the Broadway musical, "Bubbling Brown Sugar", when told to change a defective spotlight thirty-five feet above the stage floor. His supervisor provided him with a boatswain's chair, with a heavy rope to be wrapped around a hook attached to the ceiling behind the proscenium. Two co-workers pulled him up with the rope. When he was up near the bulb to be replaced, he reached out to unscrew it and slipped out of the chair. He fell 35 feet, striking the stage floor with such impact as to sustain a paralyzing neck injury.

We could not sue his employer since, under the law, Workers Compensation was his only remedy. We therefore brought suit against the famed Anta Theatre where the musical was being held, charging it with failing to provide a safe method such as a safety lift that would be part of the structure itself if needed to adjust a spotlight high above the stage.

To establish our theory, I engaged one of the finest model makers in the country, who reproduced a model that contained every finite detail of the stage and ceiling area of the Anta Theatre. In fact, it was so accurate as to contain every pulley, levy, ladder, and various other appurtenances it contained. The purpose of the model was to demonstrate that a safety lift should have been an integral part of the structure; that a simple lift with a safety cage could have avoided the tragedy that resulted in the young man being rendered a quadriplegic.

We were resisted at every turn until the day for trial actually arrived. It was then that the case was settled for $5 million.

I did not have the power to restore good health to this unfortunate young man, but at least I was able to provide him with financial security for as long as he would live.

When it was all over, I said goodbye to him and his distraught family, with tears in my eyes. I slept better that night.

MY NOVEL ACTION IN A TRAGIC CASE

As a trial lawyer, I represented many victims of tragic accidents, many of whom resulted in death. Sharing grief with families who lost a loved one due to someone's wrongful conduct was also a heartbreaker for me. I will describe just one of the many cases at this time, since new ground was broken in bringing on an action never before instituted in the nation...

Bereaved parents called my office saying it was urgent they consult with me. They had heard of my reputation and wanted to relate a tragic story that involved their sixteen-year-old son (I'll call him, "Danny"). The next day, they visited my office which occupied the entire twenty-seventh floor of the Swiss Bank building located at 222 Broadway in downtown Manhattan.

The story they related between many tears was most tragic and riveting. Since all of what follows was widely reported in the national press, in addition to a feature story published in Vanity Fair, I am not violating any confidences that would, under other circumstances, never be divulged by me.

As told to me, their sixteen-year-old son had been attending an elite summer camp located in the Northeast. Ever since he was nine years of age and having been a summer camper for all those years, the camp owners decided to confer a gift upon him by arranging that for three weeks of his last summer at the camp he would be rewarded with a trip to a number of national parks in the West, and to be chaperoned by a senior counselor. The owners also arranged for their seventeen-year-old grandson (who I will call, "Johnny") to be his roommate throughout the trip.

A complete itinerary was planned including the Grand Canyon, National Arches, Canyonlands, Zion, Bryce Canyon, and other historic national parks.

During the second week, they wound up in Flagstaff, Arizona, where a motel had been booked in advance, intending that their next visit would be to Zion National Park in Utah.

As had been the usual practice, Danny and Johnny shared the same motel room, the senior counselor being in an adjoining one. Each morning the counselor would knock on the door telling the boys to be ready for breakfast in fifteen minutes.

On this occasion, as was his custom, the counselor knocked on the door in the morning. There was no response. He knocked harder. Still, no response. Not having the room key, he proceeded downstairs and asked the room clerk to open the door to the boys' room. The two of them then proceeded to the upstairs room and the clerk opened the door with his passkey.

A HORRIFYING SCENE

When the counselor walked into the room he was horrified to see that one bed was completely soaked in blood, the other bed not having been slept in. There was a trail of blood leading from the bed to the bathroom. And there, draped over the sink was Danny, with blood all over. Danny had multiple stab wounds over his chest, back, and face. He was dead, and Johnny was nowhere to be found.

The police were immediately summoned, responded quickly and discovered a bloody knife under Danny's bed. The counselor's rented car was no longer in the parking lot outside the motel. An immediate alarm went out to find Johnny, who became the prime suspect. Failing to locate Johnny, the Flagstaff precinct received a call from his father one week later. A famous celebrity author, he advised the police that Johnny was with him and that the two of them would appear voluntarily at the stationhouse that afternoon.

When Johnny and his father arrived, they were ushered into a room by three detectives. Seated, he said that Johnny wished to make a statement and that he did not require a lawyer at the time.

A SENSELESS TRAGEDY

What followed is an unbelievable account...

Johnny stated he left the motel in the early evening, that he went to a movie, and then returned to the room. He sought out the counselor and asked to borrow the car keys so that he could listen to the radio since he was not ready to go to sleep. Innocently, the counselor gave him the key to the rental.

Johnny then proceeded to the car and listened to some music, returning about fifteen minutes later to the room he shared with Danny. By this time, Danny was fast asleep. Johnny opened the top draw of the dresser and withdrew a six inch hunting knife he had purchased at an Indian souvenir shop that afternoon. He walked quietly over to Danny's bed, raised the sharp knife high, and suddenly plunged it multiple times into Danny's chest, back, face, and other parts of his body. He then grabbed a few clothes, returned to the car and drove off heading toward the Nevada border.

As hardened as they were, the detectives were horrified by the cold-blooded killing just described by Johnny, a seventeen-year-old. Johnny was immediately arrested, given his Miranda rights, cuffed, photographed and fingerprinted. It was Johnny's father's idea (in addition to being a famous author, he was an English professor at an Ivy school), that appearing voluntarily, and making a quick confession would help in receiving youthful offender treatment from the court on behalf of his son. In such an event, he would be sentenced to a period of incarceration until he reached the age of 21, and would then be released under the supervision of a parole officer for a period of five years.

After Danny's distraught parents relayed the monstrous details surrounding the murder of their son, they asked me whether there was any civil recourse against the camp, its owners (Johnny's grandparents), or anyone else. In essence, the difficult issue was whether anyone other than the killer himself could be held civilly responsible for the tragic events that occurred.

MY CONFRONTING A NOVEL ISSUE

I advised the parents that there was no case in the country in which such a precedent had ever been established by the courts. But, without offering any promises, given my experience and instinct, I said I would bring an action against the camp, the grandfather, and Johnny's parents, only if Johnny had ever shown any violent propensity in his growing-up years. I advised them further that it was almost an impossible case to hold a parent or others civilly liable for the criminal act of a child (even at age seventeen, Johnny was considered an infant in the eyes of the law), but that I would accept the challenge. Feeling their grief over such a tragedy, I even said I would advance all litigation expenses and would receive a fee only if I was successful in settling or disposing of the case in a manner satisfactory to them if I agreed to pursue it further.

Engaging an investigative team, I learned that Johnny had psychological problems, and had exhibited some violent tendencies in the past. Buttressed with that information, I instituted a lawsuit in the federal court naming the camp, grandfather, and parents, as the defendants.

I argued to a reluctant federal judge that the actions of the defendants placed Danny at great risk by having selected Johnny to be his roommate on a three week trip out West. In fact, I was fought every inch of the way with motions to dismiss, accompanied by every trick and tool available to the defendants' law firm, a large and prestigious one.

At the end, and with a great deal of effort, time, and energy, the case was ultimately settled for a sum I cannot disclose due to the confidential agreement approved of by the federal court.

A FIRST-TIME CASE IN THE NATION

But it was the first time in the nation that such a civil action had ever been brought against a parent or others, where a child committed a criminal act. As an aside, Johnny's attempt through his lawyer to be treated as a juvenile was denied by the Arizona court. That being the case, he would be treated as an adult and as such could face the penalty of execution if convicted by a jury. To avoid that possibility, Johnny, with the advice of his attorney and father, entered a plea of guilty, in exchange for which Johnny was sentenced to life imprisonment without parole, thereby avoiding capital punishment.

A further tragedy was later reported... While serving his life sentence, Johnny confessed to a cellmate that he had murdered a young waitress in another state prior to his killing of Danny.

Making new and just law was indeed a great satisfaction, but under the horrifying and tragic circumstances, it did not serve as one of the greatest days of my life.

HE'S A SHOPLIFTER AND A THIEF

In 1985, I invited a lawyer into my office who said he had a case he would like to discuss with me, in the hope that I would agree to try it.

This is the background...

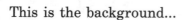

168

In 1976, two Dominican nationals (husband and wife) were visiting New York, and went to Alexander's department store in the Bronx. (Alexander's at the time was a huge retail store in the style of Macy's, but carrying a much lower end of merchandise.) They bought about one hundred dollars of goods, proceeded to the cashier, paid for their purchases and started to exit the store. When they walked through the security detectors, the loud alarms sounded. They continued onto the street, when three store security guards ran out, roughly grabbed the Dominican couple, and pulled them back into the store.

Frightened, and not knowing what was happening, the Dominican man yelled, "What's going on?" "We're charging you with shoplifting," one of the guards rang out, as husband and wife both well-dressed, were rushed into the store and thrust into a back room located on the first floor. The door was then shut and locked, and the two frightened Dominicans were kept closely guarded by the three security men.

Within a few moments, the door opened and a young man dressed in a business suit, shirt, and tie, entered. Despite the continuous protests of the Dominicans, he emptied the contents of the Alexander's bag containing the goods, seized the wallet of the Dominican man and scattered everything onto a large table. The young man also grabbed the handbag of the Dominican wife, turned it upside down with its entire contents pouring out over the top of the table as well.

Terrified, the Dominican man screamed out, "This is an insult. Everything there was paid for. What are you doing to us? You can see that the receipt is right there on the table."

Upon further inspection, the young man looked through the many garments and to his surprise discovered two shirts still with security tags attached to them, although the receipt indicated that they had been paid for. Apparently, an inexperienced cashier neglected to remove the two tags that remained on the shirts which set off the alarm as the Dominican couple were exiting the store. Their outrage was ignored since what happened to them was not an unusual occurrence with other customers when tags were not removed despite payment being made.

The Dominican couple demanded they be allowed to leave but were told they would have to wait until the chief of security returned from lunch. Despite their protests, they were restrained against their will and kept prisoners in a locked room until the chief returned one-half hour later.

When he did enter the room, and was given the information regarding the two security tags that were not removed together with the receipt showing that payment was made for every item, the Dominicans were finally allowed to leave.

A WEAK APOLOGY WAS THEIR PRACTICE

When there were similar occurrences in the past (and there were many), Alexander's, as a matter of policy would offer gift certificates valued at a few hundred dollars. If refused and a lawsuit was brought, it would usually be settled for a few thousand dollars at best. Regarding the Dominicans, they refused gift certificates and thus a lawsuit was brought against Alexander's charging it with wrongful imprisonment and assault.

During the pre-trial process and after several years, Alexander's made an offer of fifteen thousand dollars which they insisted was most generous. The offer was refused by the Dominicans despite the recommendation of their attorney that they should consider it most seriously.

In the interim, years passed, since the case was given little priority, in addition to the many adjournments granted. With that, the lawyer who filled me in with the background advised that the case had been set down "final" in three weeks and would be dismissed if the Dominican plaintiff failed to proceed to trial.

A young law clerk from my office was taking notes and at the end of our conference looked at me and whispered, "He's got to be kidding, coming here and taking up your time with such a ridiculous case." It was a typical response, spawn from both youth and inexperience. There was however, something about the matter just reported by the lawyer that was bothersome and gave me some pause.

I told him, "Before I give you an answer whether I accept this case for trial, I must meet with the Dominican couple." His response was, "They're in the Dominican Republic but I can get them here in two days."

THE CASE TAKES ON A DIFFERENT LOOK

Several days later, together with the lawyer, the Dominican couple came to my offices at 222 Broadway in downtown Manhattan. He was middle-aged, well-dressed in a dark suit, white starched shirt and conservative tie. His wife wore a stylish tailored suit, her hair was well-groomed, fingernails neatly manicured and polished. They were an attractive looking couple. What I learned in ten minutes literally knocked my socks off...

The Dominican man told me his full name was Luis Homero Lajara Burgos. He reported that the Alexander's incident occurred in 1976, that in 1978 he ran for president of the Dominican Republic but lost to a popular incumbent. It was what he then said that struck me as I immediately began to visualize a strategy that could be used in a court room.

During the 1978 campaign for the presidency, leaflets had been dropped from single engine planes over several major Dominican cities, including Santo Domingo, the largest populated city in the Dominican Republic. The headline on the pamphlets read, "Burgos Arrested For Shoplifting In New York City." Stories also appeared in the Dominican press accusing Burgos of being a thief.

Hearing all of that and seeing two very presentable people, my instinct took over as I immediately saw a different kind of trial bouncing around in my head. I told Mr. and Mrs. Burgos I would accept the case. They were overjoyed to hear my decision.

Without delay, I hit the intercom button and asked my son-in-law Jerry Parker to come to my office. When he entered, I filled him in to what my strategy would be. I needed an expert on Dominican Republic history who could be our narrator to a jury.

Within two days we located a professor (I'll call him, Professor Diaz) who had a PhD and taught a course on Dominican studies at one of the universities in New York. After conferring with him, Jerry and I were pleasantly surprised to hear he already had a fair knowledge of who Mr. Burgos was, his accomplishments and his standing within the Dominican community. He added he would do intensive research by digging into Dominican archives to prepare for his testimony.

A TRIAL OF DOMINICAN HISTORY AND INTRIGUE

When trial day arrived and Professor Diaz was called as a witness, the jury was riveted by his recitation. My whole strategy at this time was to now focus more on Burgos, the man, than on Burgos, the victim of an inexperienced Alexander's cashier. There was no issue regarding how irresponsibly he and his wife were treated by the store. The jury would have little difficulty in returning a verdict on their behalf. My focus now was upon who Mr. Burgos really was, and the loss of reputation he suffered in the Dominican Republic as a direct consequence of Alexander's wrongful conduct. Thus, what at the outset looked like a fairly garden variety case (in which Alexander's had offered fifteen thousand dollars in settlement) would now be presented to the jury as an international affair with all of its historical interest and intrigue.

As the jury leaned forward in their seats toward Professor Diaz on the witness stand, they were primed to learn the fascinating life story of Luis Homero Lajera Burgos which they were about to hear.

For two days, Professor Diaz provided the intimate details of the rise of Burgos, the son of a peasant farmer who became a candidate for the Presidency of the Dominican Republic. It was a remarkable human interest story. In finite detail, the jury listened with awe as they heard how a young man enlisted in the army; rose up through the ranks; was the victim of a political arrest by the then Dominican dictator Raphael Trujillo; jailed without a trial; spent years in prison; how upon his release he organized the peasants throughout the country giving them a voice of protest they never had; how he was appointed to the police bureau; how he rose through the ranks to become the chief police enforcement officer; how he was designated by the President to head an armada of sailing ships to Spain replaying in reverse the exploration by Spain of the

Dominican Republic in 1492; how he was greeted by Francisco Franco, Spain's military dictator and presented with Spain's highest honors; and how he was even knighted.

The narrative continued with a gripping historical back story describing each event. The jury, and even the judge, were glued to their seats as Professor Diaz related drama after drama about the rise of Burgos that the professor had compiled from ancient documents he discovered in the Dominican archives. Each account was so immersed in human interest that any by itself could have served as the plot of a thriller movie. When finished with his testimony, the jury viewed Burgos in a completely different light which of course was the strategy that my assistant Jerry Parker and I had crafted from the start.

I even made arrangements for a former Dominican Secretary of State to come to the New York courtroom, who when called as a witness, attested to an airplane dropping leaflets over Santo Domingo and other cities and who also confirmed the testimony of Professor Diaz regarding Burgos, his reputation and standing.

In addition to being manhandled by Alexander's security detail and held prisoner for more than an hour, we claimed that the loss of Mr. Burgos' reputation was irreparable, an added factor that cost him the election for President of the Dominican Republic.

WE THE JURY FIND...

At the end, the jury retired to deliberate its verdict. Three hours later they returned to the courtroom. A verdict had been reached. The foreman stood up and reported it. "We, the jury, find for the plaintiff in the sum of one million dollars." It was the highest verdict ever recorded in a shoplifting case. In fact, the *New York Times* and every newspaper in New York featured the story the next day.

The verdict and its record amount were most gratifying, but even such a satisfying victory did not rise to being the greatest day of my life.

TRAGEDY REPLACES JOY

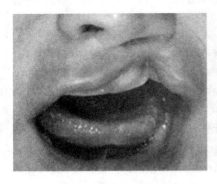

Unfortunately, some of the roads of life lead to tragedy. We as humans have no explanation although many theories abound. Somehow, despair has its own formula in replacing joy, and oftentimes with little warning. When that occurs, all we as mortals can do is pray, as would believers in the deity, or live in the hope that in the end, everything will turn out right, all of which takes me to a most heart breaking story...

I'll call her Baby Mary. She was born with a cleft palate, a not too uncommon condition in which the palate in utero does not form properly during the early stages of pregnancy. The cause is not scientifically established, with more than 200,000 cases per year in the United States alone. In essence, a cleft palate is a birth condition that leaves an opening in the roof of the newborn's mouth, or it may leave an opening in both the lip as well as the roof.

Baby Mary was a beautiful one-year-old, born with both conditions. It was a disorder that if untreated, could result in feeding, speech, and other serious problems. A surgical repair within 18 months of birth is usually successful and should always be sought.

Within the appropriate window, Baby Mary was admitted into a local hospital where a highly-trained pediatric surgeon performed the cleft palate surgery consistent with appropriate surgical standards. The operation was a success, and the happy parents were relieved that all went so well in the OR.

Following surgery, the inside of Baby Mary's mouth was packed with gauze to absorb the bleeding expected from such a procedure. This is the terrible sequence that followed...

Unbeknown to the nursing staff, one of the pieces of gauze freed itself from the wound site and began to migrate downward toward Baby Mary's windpipe. Tragically, sometime later, the baby went into cardiac arrest as a result of the gauze pad that significantly blocked air and oxygen from passing through. When this catastrophe was discovered, the code was immediately sounded as doctors and staff rushed in and quickly removed the gauze blocking the windpipe. They were able to revive Baby Mary, but the absence of oxygen to the brain for an extended period caused permanent brain damage.

Although Baby Mary was spared from death, the poor child would suffer severe disability for the rest of her life. The devastation to her parents was without measure. Despite the settlement of $5.2 million (20 years ago), no dollar amount could ever restore their beautiful baby to a life of quality that was ripped away so unexpectedly.

Baby Mary's life, and that of her distraught parents, began a journey on the road of sadness, and one they did not deserve. Again, as in so many disasters throughout the world, tragedy replaced joy, as we compassionate humans sit by and wonder why.

TWO DIFFERENT WORLDS

It was the fall of 2005 and as usual, the terminal at the San Diego airport was busy that morning. I sat down in the only remaining empty seat in the gate area waiting to board the plane to Fort Myers, Florida. There was a young man seated to my left, duffel bag between his legs. He couldn't have been more than 18, maybe 19.

"How ya doin?" I asked, trying to be casual and friendly. "OK," he answered, shyly.

"Where you off to?"

"Going home on a 10-day furlough."

During the next half hour, until the announcement to board came, I learned much about the young man. In his high school senior year, a Marine recruiting team stationed outside the school pitched enlistments to all who paused long enough to listen.

"You'll get a sign-up bonus. We'll even send you to college and pay for it. You'll learn a career while serving your country." And so on.

In short time, the spit and polish recruiting sergeant dressed in spiffy blues, joined by a one-striper in a starched shirt and sharply creased trousers, sought out my young friend each day after school. Within a week, they sold him on a four-year enlistment with all the bells and whistles they said went with the deal. His parents, who migrated to the United States 12 years earlier, were asked by their son to give consent. They were too upset to say "yes," but too proud to say "no." Instead they remained silent, even as their son was sworn into service and later sent to Parris Island for his basic training.

"Where will you go after your 10-day leave?" "It's back to the coast," he answered.

"And then?"

"I'm shipping out to Iraq."

"He's just a kid," I thought. *"Life hasn't even started for him, and soon he'll be fighting a war in a very dangerous place"*—a war that most Americans are almost unaffected by.

It's as if we at home live in two different worlds. Life in one goes on—our job, family, friends, school, big league sports, movies, vacations, fun—and yet there's another world we see from a distance on a TV news screen: The world of war, fear, horror, killing—the death of almost 2,300 of our finest young Americans; the wrenching pain of their loved ones; more than 25,000 wounded, many without limbs, most with broken bodies, damaged minds, and the countless deaths of innocent civilians caught in the crossfire. We then channel-surf to some banal sitcom, "business as usual"—and "have a nice day".

I remember coming back to the states from overseas duty after almost four years of World War II service and being treated as if I were a hero—a sense that folks appreciated whatever sacrifices were made for our country.

Can the same be said today?

I knew the young Marine was at the bottom rung of the pay ladder, so I asked whether he received a military discount for his air tickets. "No," was his reply. The irony was that he paid even more for his ticket than I for mine since he booked later than I did. In fact, he couldn't even get a confirmed seat for his trip home and had to go standby. Fortunately, his name was announced by the flight agent.

Soon we started to board. His seat was many rows behind mine, but as we took off, I thought, *"Why aren't we as involved with his world of war as we were with another war 60 years earlier?"*

We finally touched down at Southwest Florida International Airport. Shortly after that, I was seated comfortably in front of my high-definition, flat screen TV watching 18 grown men play a kid's game, as tons of fans roared in the stands, eating hot dogs and drinking beer.

At the same moment, there were other kids—thousands of them—in a far more dangerous game, 7,000 miles from home. It made me think more about our two worlds, how they got started, and how separated they really were. The more I thought about it, the sadder I became. And somehow, it just didn't seem right.

Six months later, I read his name in a newspaper. His lightly armored truck was blown up by a roadside bomb outside of Baghdad. My young friend died in his world. Our world barely noticed.

With my former professor and new partner Alfred S. Julien, Esq., after I resigned from the New York State Supreme Court.

Being back in the practice of law as a trial lawyer, I am walking down the steps of the Manhattan Supreme Court, located at 60 Centre Street, in New York City.

I am in my study at home. The Lincoln bookends were presented to me as a gift by a grateful client.

NEWSDAY, SUNDAY, JULY 22, 1979

Ex-Judge on Other Side of Bar

By Edward Hershey

"To be a judge, you've got to have a very deep sense of justice, a sense of what is right, just, fair and even-handed. The role of a lawyer is quite different. You are an advocate, an adversary and a combatant in every sense of the word."

—Former Judge
Leonard Finz

A Newsday article. 1979.

A Former Queens Judge Triumphs as a Lawyer

A former Queens judge, who left the bench in January to resume his law practice because he said he couldn't make ends meet on his $49,000-a-year judicial salary, has won a $1.5-million malpractice suit for a client represented by his firm. He said that the award is believed to be one of the largest of its kind in state history.

The award was made Wednesday by a State Supreme Court jury in Schenectady to 60-year-old Ann Tuccillo, who has been paralyzed from the neck down since 1969, when she was injected with an antihistamine and adrenalin for hives while a patient at St. Clare's Hospital in Schenectady. It was not known whether the hospital would appeal the verdict.

Former Judge Leonard Finz of Little Neck, who argued the case, said that Mrs. Tuccillo had gone to the emergency room of the hospital for treatment of hives. She was admitted as a patient. Seven hours later, she had an outbreak of hives, and the nurse on duty called the doctor who had treated her in the emergency room.

Finz said that the doctor instructed the nurse to administer the injection, which, Finz contended at the trial, caused a massive stroke or blood clot in the brain. That was diagnosed only when Mrs. Tuccillo was sent to Columbia Presbyterian Hospital in Manhattan, he said.

Five minutes after the injection, Finz said, Mrs. Tuccillo had gone into a coma, and did not come out of it for three months. Finz said that although Mrs. Tuccillo had a history of cardiac problems, her blood pressure and heart were not routinely monitored. Mrs. Tuccillo is now a resident in an Albany nursing home.

Finz, who served on the bench for 13 years, said he stepped down because his judicial salary was not meeting the expenses involved in putting his two children through college. He joined a Manhattan law firm as a partner.

—Alison Mitchell

A Newsday article. 1978.

$1.5 Million Awarded in a Hives Malpractice Sui

By MAX H. SEIGEL

A 51-year-old woman who entered a Schenectady, N.Y., hospital suffering from hives and left the hospital paralyzed from the neck down was awarded $1.5 million in a medical malpractice suit last week.

Court sources said it was the highest award won in New York State in a suit against a hospital by an individual.

After a jury in State Supreme Court in Schenectady County announced its verdict last Wednesday, the trial judge, J. Raymond Amyot, interjected a new legal problem when he asked the jury to apportion the percentage of fault.

The jury held the defendant, St. Claire's Hospital, responsible for 50 percent and two physicians responsible for the other 50 percent.

Leonard L. Finz of the firm of Julien

Amyot's action in asking for an apportionment of fault.

The plaintiff, Ann Tuccillo, had entered St. Claire's Hospital on Nov. 30, 1969, suffering from hives. She was examined by an intern, employed by the hospital, and by a private physician, according to testimony.

Medication Contained Cortisone

The woman was then admitted as a patient and given intravenous medication containing cortisone, testimony at the trial indicated. In addition, she was given

an injection of epinephrine, a medication said to be similar to adrenalin, according to the testimony.

Mrs. Tuccillo showed signs of recovery for about six hours, her lawyer said, and then the nurse on duty noticed the hives returning.

The testimony showed that the nurse then called the intern and without examining the patient, he ordered two drugs administered. They were benadryl, an antihistimine, and epinephrine. Five minutes after the injections, Mrs. Tuccillo went into a deep coma. She remained in a coma at St. Claire's for five weeks, until

Schlesinger & Finz, who represented the plaintiff, noted that the two physician Dr. Joseph Vacca and Dr. Stephen Se had previously settled claims again them for $100,000 and had been droppe as defendants in the case.

"Since they were no longer defendant how could they be assessed damages t the jury?" the lawyer, a former state S preme Court Justice in Queens, aske Mr. Finz said he would appeal Justi

Jan. 6, 1970, when she was transferre to the Columbia Presbyterian Hospital I New York City.

Tests there, the testimony showed, di closed that she had sustained a bloo clot that blocked the main artery feedin the stem of the brain, destroying par of the brain and causing her paralysi "She was a living tomb buried aliv within her own body," Mr. Finz sai Lawyers for St. Claire's have contende during the trial that Mrs. Tuccillo ha suffered a stroke that had no relatio to any injection of drugs.

A New York Times article. 1978.

A New Legal Tactic in the Fight To Compensate Victims of DES

By NADINE BROZAN

Joyce Bichler wept on the witness stand as she described the ways that having a hysterectomy and vaginectomy at age 18 had affected her life. Her mother, her father and some of the spectators in the State Supreme Court in the Bronx yesterday cried openly too.

Miss Bichler, now a 25-year-old social worker who helps the "frail elderly" in San Francisco, has, for the moment, taken center stage in the ongoing controversy over diethylstilbestrol, a synthetic estrogen that has been definitively linked to one form of cancer in the daughters of some women who took it to avert a miscarriage.

Last month, in a decision similar to those rendered in other such cases, a jury decided that Miss Bichler had not adequately proved that Eli Lilly & Company had produced the specific prescription given to her mother 25 years ago to prevent staining, which she had experienced during two prior successful pregnancies. Four weeks ago, Miss Bichler went back into court in her lawsuit against the same company but using a different and as yet untested legal approach, that of joint enterprise liability.

Its premise is that because so many manufacturers produced the drug in generically identical form and that because inadequate record keeping has made it virtually impossible to trace the origins of specific prescriptions, all manufacturers can be held culpable. Nevertheless, only the Lilly Company is the target in this case because the plaintiff contends the drug maker was a major and early producer of the estrogen. The joint enterprise principle was recently ruled viable for trial in a California appellate court in a case involving the drug.

Diethylstilbestrol, more commonly called DES, has been prescribed for many purposes including, ironically the treatment of some forms of cancer. In 1947, it was given Food and Drug Administration approval for use in cases of threatened miscarriage. In 1952, reports began to surface that indicated the drug was ineffective for that purpose, but there was no major public outcry over the drug's risks until 1971. That year a Boston physician

> **DES is a major issue for women's health activist groups.**

reported that seven daughters of New England residents who had taken the estrogen had developed clear cell adenocarcinoma, a previously almost nonexistent form of glandular cancer of the vagina. Subsequently, the F.D.A. began requiring that product labels state that DES was contraindicated for use in the prevention of miscarriage. By that time, DES had been taken by an estimated 500,000 to two million women.

In the last four years, DES has become a major issue for women's health activist organizations. (Yesterday representatives of the National Organization for Women, the Women's Counseling Service at Barnard College, the National Women's Health Network and DES Action National attended the trial to distribute leaflets outside the courthouse and to give Miss Bichler their support inside.) The Department of Health, Education and Welfare convened a DES Task Force in February 1978, which issued a major report in September confirming that the drug is linked to clear cell adenocarcinoma among daughters of women who had taken DES and suggested it might be responsible for other abnormalities in the women who had taken it and in their sons, too. Many DES daughters have been found to have adaenosis, the presence of nonmalignant glandular tissue in the vagina. Other research is now under way and New York, for one, has begun a program to locate the children of the estimated 100,000 women in the state who took DES. The state is sponsoring eight diagnostic centers, five of which are in the metropolitan area.

So far, no women have won a DES case in court. Although a number of lawsuits, both individual and class action, have been filed, most have been admitted to trial because of difficulty in identifying specific manufacturers in each case. About 300 companies

made the drug at one time or another over the years. Lawyers and pharmaceutical executives are keeping a close eye on the Bichler case: if the joint enterprise liability approach prevails, manufacturers could conceivably be held responsible for damages without proof that they had produced the drug in question.

Justice Arnold G. Fraiman cautioned Miss Bichler's lawyer, Leonard L. Finz, himself a former New York State Supreme Court Justice, that he would have to offer compelling logic for that argument. The defense was to begin presenting its arguments yesterday, and although its primary lawyer, Russel Beatie, would not comment on the case outside the courtroom, he did suggest in court that at the time Mrs. Bichler took the drug there was absolutely no evidence to create suspicion that it might be carcinogenic.

Miss Bichler is the daughter of a retired New York City firefighter. She is also a Phi Beta Kappa graduate of the State University of New York at Stony Brook.

She recalled how after the removal of her uterus, two-thirds of her vagina, lymph glands, and one ovary in a five-hour operation in Albert Einstein College Hospital seven years ago, she had tried to terminate her 6-month-old relationship with Michael Kimbarow, then a 19-year-old student and now a speech pathologist. "I couldn't believe that he still wanted to love me, so I had to test him, although I wasn't aware that that was what I was doing. I did everything I could to send him away."

"I love Michael, and I will never be able to give him a child," she said, sobbing and looking straight at the slender young man she had married in March 1976.

The case is expected to go to the jury in about 10 days.

A New York Times article. 1979.

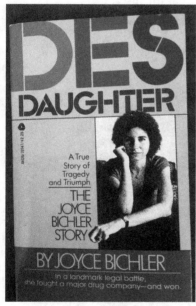

The book cover of, "DES Daughter", by my client, Joyce Bichler.

With Phil Donahue taken in the green room prior to a live TV interview.

New York Law Journal

Tuesday, September 30, 1997

$5.2 Million Accord In Brain-Damage Case

A $5.2 million settlement was reported yesterday on behalf of an 8-year-old girl who suffered brain damage following surgery to repair a cleft palate.

The settlement, reached during a trial in Brooklyn Supreme Court, involved claims that Lisa DelSante, then 1 year old, suffered the injuries from deprivation of oxygen when she went into cardiac arrest 40 hours after surgery and initial attempts at resuscitation were unsuccessful. The incident occurred at Brookdale Hospital, while she was under the care of its nursing staff.

The plaintiff was represented by Leonard L. Finz and Michael A. Carlucci of Finz & Finz; the hospital by Warren Sanger of Bower, Sanger & Futterman; a surgeon by Robert Whittaker of Martin Clearwater & Bell; and a duty nurse by Irving Hirsch of Wilson, Elser, Moskowitz, Edelman & Dicker. The settlement was reached before Justice William Bellard.

A New York Law Journal article describing the, "Baby Mary", settlement.

Award cancer victim 500G in DES suit

By PETER McLAUGHLIN

A Bronx Supreme Court jury awarded a 25-year-old woman $300,000 yesterday in her damage suit against the Eli Lilly Co., which produced DES, a synthetic estrogen that has been linked to cancer in daughters of some women who took it during pregnancies.

It is believed to be the first jury award in the country in a suit involving DES.

The jury of three men and three women deliberated five days before finding in favor of the plaintiff, Joyce Bichler, a social worker.

At the six-week trial, Bichler contended that she suffered a form of cancer because her mother used DES during pregnancy to prevent miscarriage. In a cancer operation performed seven years ago at Albert Einstein College Hospital, Bichler suffered removal of her uterus, two-thirds of her vagina, lymph glands and one ovary.

"Landmark decision"

Outside court, one of the jurors told reporters: "We finally decided that if the company had done the proper testing, they would have seen that the drug caused cancer."

Bichler's lawyer, former Queens Supreme Court Justice Leonard Finz, called the verdict a "landmark decision."

"For the first time in history," he said, "a jury brought a verdict against an industry" which failed "to adequately test DES in the animal laboratory before placing it in the bodies of helpless pregnant women."

"I feel wonderful," Bichler said. "My primary concern was the verdict, not the money. The verdict affects everyone."

A spokesman for Lilly said the Indianapolis-based firm would appeal. "We believe this verdict is contrary to law and won't be sustained on appeal. It was never proved that Lilly made the drug taken by Bichler's mother, but the company was the largest distributor of DES.

A news article, and a telegram received from dear friends, following the DES verdict. 1979.

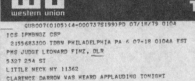

western union — Telegram

QUB007(0105)(4-000737S199)PD 07/18/79 0104

ICS IPMBNGZ CSP
2155683300 TDBN PHILADELPHIA PA 6 07-18 0104A EST
PMS JUDGE LEONARD FINZ, DLR
5327 254 ST
LITTLE NECK NY 11362
CLARENCE DARROW WAS HEARD APPLAUDING TONIGHT
GLORIA AND LARRY
NNNN

NEW YORK POST

FRIDAY, MAY 25, 1979   25 CENTS   © 1979 News Group Publications, Inc.   Vol. 178. No. 163

First suit by DES baby may set legal standard

By JAMI BERNARD and Al SOSTCHEN

A woman who developed vaginal cancer 18 years after her mother took a controversial hormone during pregnancy has filed a $30 million suit against the pharmaceutical company that made the drug.

It is the first such suit to be brought in New York State involving the drug diethylstilbestrol, better known as DES.

Joyce Bichler, 26, is suing the Eli Lilly Co. of Indianapolis, which supplied the DES pills that her mother, Dorothy, took in 1953. Miss Bichler developed cancer of the vagina and cervix at 18, while she was a student at Stony Brook State University.

DES, a synthetic hormonal drug prescribed for pregnant women from 1940 to 1970 to prevent miscarriage, was taken off the market when it was linked to cancer in the female children of women who took it.

The decision in the trial in Bronx Supreme Court before Judge Arnold G. Fraiman, could have widespread ramifications. At least 100,000 women in New York State alone were exposed to the drug during pregnancy.

Miss Bichler underwent surgery to "stabilize" her condition, but suffers from cosmetic disfigurement, psychological trauma, depression, and may be unable to bear children, according to her lawyer, Leonard Finz.

Because of insufficient data on DES babies and the uncertainty of the future, he says his client is living with a "time bomb."

Finz claims Eli Lilly Co. played "a leadership role in getting approval of the FDA for marketing of the drug in 1941.

"The FDA relied heavily on the research and literature supplied by Lilly in approving the drug for marketing," said Finz.

He claimed that the company did not test the product sufficiently despite researchers' warnings that the drug caused cancer in animals.

Lilly's lawyer, Russell Beatty, contends in court papers that DES had not been proven to cause cancer in female offspring, and that its harm could not have been predicted back in 1953 when Dorothy Bichler took the drug.

Post Photo By Jerry Engel

Joyce Bichler (right) claims in suit that her cancerous condition was a result of her mother, Dorothy (left), using the drug DES during pregnancy.

A New York Post article. 1979.

New York Post, and New York Times articles describing DES issues. 1979.

N.Y. Post July 17, 1979

Jury faults tests in 500G DES award

By AL SOSTCHEN

THE FIRST verdict ever in favor of a DES victim "was not made because of sympathy," a juror told The Post today.

The verdict yesterday, which awarded $500,000 to a Bronx woman who contracted vaginal cancer 18 years after her mother took the drug to avoid a miscarriage, could have nationwide repercussions.

"We were hung up until we decided that if they [the drug company] did the proper testing, they would have foreseen that this drug caused cancer," said the male juror.

"Sympathy for the defendant had nothing to do with it."

Joyce Bichler, now a 25-year-old social worker, wept as the foreman of the three-man and three-woman jury announced the unanimous Bronx Supreme Court verdict yesterday against Eli Lilly Co.

Lilly, one of the country's leading drug companies, is expected to appeal.

Outside the courtroom, Miss Bichler held her head in her hands and sobbed hysterically. "It showed that they can't do this to us. They can't do this to us. They can't use us as guinea pigs.

"I never did this just for myself. I did it for every body, for every consumer faced by this terrible thing so they could fight back."

The jurors deliberated

JOYCE BICHLER
'They can't do this to us.'

for five days after a grueling, complex six-week trial before Justice Arnold Fraiman.

"We were hung up on whether there was proper testing by the company," said the same juror.

The verdict made new law and could result in a flood of similar actions across the country by "DES babies."

Miss Bichler had sued for $5 million.

Unable to prove that the company produced the prescription filled for the mother, the plaintiff sued on the untested grounds of "joint enterprise liability."

Former Supreme Court Justice Leonard L. Finz, lawyer for Miss Bichler, contended that all manufacturers of DES could be held culpable, and that the Lilly Co. was targeted because it was an early major producer (over 40 per cent) of the drug.

Woman Wins Suit In DES Case

By NADINE BROZAN

In a groundbreaking verdict rendered yesterday in the State Supreme Court in the Bronx, a jury decided that a pharmaceutical company must pay $500,000 in damages to a woman for cancer caused by DES, a drug given to her mother to prevent miscarriage, even though the victim failed to establish which company had actually manufactured the doses in question.

The verdict marked the first time that a woman had won a lawsuit involving DES, which stands for diethylstilbestrol. The decision was regarded as a victory in the women's health movement and certain to bolster the morale of women around the country who had previously sued without success in various courts. DES has been linked to cancer of offspring in scattered cases and has also reportedly caused thousands of cases of adenosis — the abnormal presence of nonmalignant glandular tissue in the vagina.

In the Bronx case, the jury rendered judgment against Eli Lilly & Company in favor of Joyce Bichler, a 25-year-old social worker. Russ Durbin, a spokesman at Lilly headquarters in Indianapolis, said, "We believe this verdict is contrary to the law and won't be sustained on appeal. We do plan to appeal."

Seven years ago, Miss Bichler, who is married but uses her maiden name, underwent a hysterectomy and vaginectomy at the Albert Einstein College Hospital. Her mother was given the drug because her doctor feared a possible miscarriage. The synthetic estrogen was widely administered during 1940's and 1950's and even later for that purpose.

Earlier Suits Dismissed

This spring Miss Bichler sued Eli Lilly but, as in previous cases, whether individual lawsuits or class actions, the suit was dismissed for lack of proof that a specific manufacturer had produced the specific medication taken by Miss Bichler's mother, Dorothy. The Lilly Company was the target of the suit because the plaintiff contended that the drug maker was major and early producer of DES.

Miss Bichler's lawyer, Leonard L. Finz, a former New York State Supreme Court Justice, decided to pursue the case on an untested legal premise: that of joint enterprise liability or common responsibility for adequate testing and safety control procedures among manufacturers, an approach that had the drug industry and the legal community watching the case closely.

The jury, three men and three women, which had deliberated for five days, an unusually lengthy period for a civil case, had to answer seven questions — written by the presiding justice, Arnold G. Fraiman — in order to reach a verdict:

¶ Was DES safe for miscarriage purposes in 1953, (the year Miss Bichler's mother was given DES for two or three weeks)?

¶ Did DES cause Miss Bichler's vaginal and cervical cancer?

¶ In 1953, should a reasonably prudent drug manufacturer have foreseen that DES might cause cancer in the offspring of pregnant women who took it?

¶ Foreseeing that DES might cause cancer in the offspring of pregnant women who took it, would a prudent drug manufacturer test it on pregnant mice before marketing it?

¶ If DES had been tested on pregnant mice, would the tests have shown that DES caused cancer in their offspring?

¶ Would a prudent manufacturer have marketed DES for miscarriage purposes in 1953 had it known that it caused cancer in the offspring of pregnant mice?

¶ Did the defendant, Eli Lilly, and the other drug manufacturers act in concert with each other in the testing and marketing of DES for miscarriage purposes?

According to Mr. Finz, the jury had to find for the plaintiff on each of the seven questions and on all but two, it ruled unanimously. One juror dissented on the matter of safety for mis-

> A jury decided that Eli Lilly should pay $500,000 to a woman whose mother had taken the drug.

carriage and the responsibility of the drug for Miss Bichler's cancer.

Just after the jury announced its verdict, Mr. Finz said, "This is an absolute victory in every sense. From this day forward, the standards in the drug industry will have to be high to ensure that every drug marketed is safe and effective."

In addition to being a cause of cancer, DES was long ago shown to be ineffective as a miscarriage preventative, one point that was emphasized by Miss Bichler's lawyer during the eight-week trial.

Fran Fishbane, president of DES Action, National, an organization of individuals exposed to the drug, and other concerned citizens, said, "If the pharmaceutical companies had established a fund for the DES-exposed when they discovered the risk to cancer (in 1971), they would not now have to worry about the flood of lawsuits that are due to come. I expect they will be swamped."

Lawrence S. Charfoos, a Detroit lawyer who specializes in product liability and malpractice litigation and who presently has DES cases pending in 18 states, said of the verdict, "It can only be good for the young women of America, and from a negotiating and settlement point of view, it has some value. But," he emphasized, "no trial-level case sets a precedent. It will have to be affirmed on the appellate level.

Joyce Bichler said, "This verdict is not just for me but for all American consumers."

New York Law Journal

SERVING THE BENCH AND BAR SINCE 1888

NEW YORK, TUESDAY, JULY 17, 1979

Jury Puts Liability On Drug Industry For Woman's Cancer

In what is believed to be the first such finding in the country placing liability upon the entire pharmaceutical industry, a Bronx jury yesterday awarded $500,000 to a twenty-five-year-old woman who, it decided, contracted vaginal cancer as the result of drug DES which had been administered to her mother during pregnancy.

The six-member jury in Bronx Supreme Court issued what trial attorneys are calling a landmark verdict on the novel legal theory of joint enterprise liability — holding the entire pharmaceutical industry liable because the drug, Diethylstilbestrol, or DES, was manufactured generically, preventing individual liability. DES was widely distributed in the '40s and '50s to prevent miscarriages.

Novel Jury Verdict

Leon L. Finz, of Julien, Schlesinger and Finz, counsel for plaintiff Joyce Bichler, said he believed the verdict was the first by a jury on the question of joint enterprise liability. Justice Arnold Guy Fraiman presided over the two-month trial. The theory has been upheld on summary judgment motions in California and in Federal court in

Brooklyn, but never at the jury level.

The named defendant in the half-million-dollar award was Eli Lilly and Company, which had taken the lead in the research and production of DES more than thirty years ago. Mr. Finz, who is a former Supreme Court justice in Queens, noted that a suit earlier this year seeking to hold Eli Lilly individually responsible was unsuccessful because of the drug's generic production. It was then that the joint enterprise liability approach was introduced, and permitted by Justice Fraiman.

7 Questions Posed

The jury issued its unanimous finding after answering seven special interrogatories on liability. The interrogatories dealt with the failure of a "prudent drug manufacturer" to have tested DES, a synthetic estrogen, on mice, before its distribution, and to have known it could cause cancer in the daughters of mothers who took it.

Ms. Bichler, who is married but uses her maiden name, developed vaginal cancer in 1972 and underwent surgery, including a radical hysterectomy and a vaginectomy. Her mother, Dorothy, had received DES in 1953 while pregnant with Joyce.

Wide Interest

The legal and insurance communities were watching the two-month trial closely because of the ramifications of joint enterprise liability. Not only will the jury verdict give thousands of other women who were affected by the drug an opportunity for bringing their own actions, but it could open the way for suits involving not only the pharmaceutical industry but for product liability cases on a generic basis affecting a broad spectrum of manufacturers, according to legal observers.

As for DES itself, the Federal Food and Drug Administration estimates that between 1947 and 1971, between 500,000 to 3 million pregnant women took the drug as miscarriage prevention. In New York alone, it is estimated that there were 100,000 women who took DES. The state is operating eight diagnostic centers for daughters of these women.

Eli Lilly could, if it so chooses, seek apportionment of the verdict among other manufacturers of DES, on the basis of *Dole v. Dow*. It has this alternative available, according to observers, because the jury found that all had acted in concert in establishing an insufficient, industry-wide standard of safety, forming the basis for joint enterprise liability.

The trial came close to ending in a mistrial last Friday when one of the jurors after three days of deliberations, collapsed because of high blood pressure and the "tension" of reaching a verdict.

Justice Fraiman, who was involved in a controversial ruling from the State Court of Appeals earlier in the week for his premature granting of a mistrial in a 1975 criminal case, recessed the trial for the weekend. The jury returned its verdict yesterday afternoon.

In addition to Mr. Finz, Ms. Bichler, who is now a social worker in San Francisco, was represented by Edward J. Sanocki Jr. and Sybil Shainwald, also of Julien, Schlesinger; Eli Lilly by Russell Brettle and William Drauer, of Dewey, Ballantine Bushby, Palmer & Wood.

A New York Law Journal article describing the DES case that ultimately went up to the United States Supreme Court. 1979.

DAILY ⊙ NEWS

NEW YORK, WEDNESDAY, MAY 12, 1982   Mostly sunn

New York Times article, and Daily News article, describing the winning appeal by New York's highest court in the Joyce Bichler DES case. 1979.

The New York Times

WEDNESDAY, MAY 12, 1982
Copyright © 1982 The New York Times

State High Court Upholds Woman In Case Involving Cancer and DES

By E. R. SHIPP

New York State's highest court yesterday upheld a damage award against a manufacturer of the drug DES, even though the plaintiff could not prove that the company had produced the DES that she said had caused her cancer.

The tribunal, the State Court of Appeals, unanimously upheld a theory of liability that had led to a $492,000 judgment against the manufacturer, Eli Lilly & Company of Indianapolis. Lower courts had said that the cancer victim, Joyce Bichler, was not required to identify positively the company that produced the DES that affected her.

Instead, they said, she could sue any company that had manufactured and marketed the drug between 1947, when it was first approved for the prevention of miscarriages, and 1971, when it was declared unsafe for pregnant women.

The courts found. Ily liable because it was one of a dozen companies that had engaged in a "concerted action" to win Federal approval of the drug and to market it without either testing it or heeding studies that as early as 1938 warned of possible harm from the use of DES during pregnancy.

DES, which is short for diethylstilbestrol, is a synthetic estrogen made from coal-tar derivatives and sold as a generic drug. It is still being marketed for other uses, but the Federal Food and Drug Administration withdrew its approval for its use in pregnant women in 1971. Miss Bichler, who is 28 years old and lives in Minnesota, was born in the Bronx; her mother took the drug while she was pregnant.

According to the court, about 1,000 lawsuits have since been filed against DES manufacturers. In its opinion, written by Associate Judge Bernard S. Meyer, it said, "With the passage of the many years needed for DES-caused vaginal tract abnormalities to appear in prenatally exposed offspring, the patient, physician, pharmacist and drug-company records which could have identified the source of the DES have usually disappeared."

The opinion continued: "Products-liability law cannot be expected to stand still where innocent victims face inordinately difficult problems of proof."

Uphold 500G award in DES cancer case

By DON SINGLETON

The state's highest court ruled yesterday that the Eli Lilly pharmaceutical company must pay $500,000 to a woman who developed cancer as a teenager because her mother had taken the anti-miscarriage drug DES.

The woman's attorneys, former Queens Supreme Court Justice Leonard L. Finz and Alfred S. Julien, called the case a landmark, since the award was made although there was no proof that Lilly actually manufactured the DES pills taken by the mother of the victim, Joyce Bichler.

Lilly was, however, the largest of several United States manufacturers of DES. The drug was used in the late 1940s and 1950s to prevent miscarriages and other female reproductive problems, but was banned in 1971 as a possible threat to the health of unborn children.

In yesterday's unanimous ruling, the Court of Appeals upheld a 1979 Bronx Supreme Court award to Bichler, whose mother took DES in 1953 shortly before Bichler was born. Bichler, a social worker who now lives in Minnesota, developed vaginal and cervical cancer when she was 17. As a result, she was forced to undergo removal of all her reproductive organs and half of her vagina.

In a statement issued yesterday afternoon, Lilly said it was "appalled" by the decision. ■

Leonard Finz

DES Claims Reach Third Generation

In 1954 Marsha Kanarek took the drug DES to help prevent a miscarriage. Thirty-one years later, her granddaughter Amy was born with cerebral palsy. The child's mother, ▓▓▓▓▓▓ ▓▓▓▓▓▓, was convinced there was a link.

▓▓▓▓ turned to New York-based plaintiffs' lawyer Leonard Finz, a former New York state supreme court justice who won the first verdict ever returned for a DES daughter, in 1979. In what appears to be the first third-generation DES liability suit, ▓▓▓▓ is suing seven former DES-producing drug companies on behalf of her 19-month-old daughter. The suit asks for $100 million in damages.

The grandmother's use of DES "created an anatomically deficient uterus" in the mother, contends Finz, which in turn led to a tragic, premature birth. ▓▓▓▓ has a T-shaped uterus, as opposed to a normal pear-shaped one, and therefore could not carry her baby to full term.

The scenario is not uncommon, says Finz, adding that 90 percent of DES daughters have malformed uteruses and vaginas: "[There is a] very strong possibility of having literally hundreds of thousands of third-generation cases."

DES was given to 6 million expectant mothers between 1947 and 1971, before evidence of links to cancer led to its removal from the market. Noting the demographic possibilities, Finz exclaims, "The geometrical procession is just frightening."

As for DES producers, Finz says, third-generation suits could "potentially expose [them] to billions and billions of dollars [in claims]." —*Robert Safian*

An article in "The American Lawyer" describing a novel legal concept. Circa 1990s.

I am being met by members of the press following the winning verdict in the DES case.

The press interviews me outside of the courtroom after a winning verdict in one of my cases that made national news.

This shows the back of the media. I am in the middle of the photo.

I am sitting in my study at home after a six-week trial that made national news.

This is a press conference dealing with a front page story that involved a New York State Supreme Court Justice.

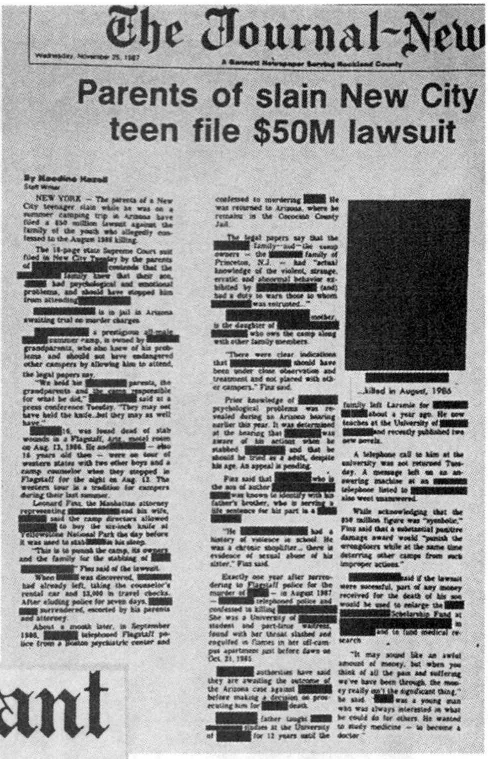

The Journal-News

Wednesday, November 25, 1987 — A Gannett Newspaper Serving Rockland County

Parents of slain New City teen file $50M lawsuit

By Naedine Hazell
Staff Writer

NEW YORK — The parents of a New City teenager slain while he was on a summer camping trip in Arizona have filed a $50 million lawsuit against the family of the youth who allegedly confessed to the August 1986 killing.

The 18-page state Supreme Court suit filed in New City Tuesday by the parents of [redacted] contends that the [redacted] family knew that their son, [redacted] had psychological and emotional problems, and should have stopped him from attending [redacted]

[redacted] is in jail in Arizona awaiting trial on murder charges.

[redacted] a prestigious all-male [redacted] summer camp, is owned by [redacted] grandparents, who also knew of his problems and should not have endangered other campers by allowing him to attend, the legal papers say.

"We hold his [redacted] parents, the grandparents and the camp responsible for what he did," [redacted] said at a press conference Tuesday. "They may not have held the knife...but they may as well have."

[redacted] 16, was found dead of stab wounds in a Flagstaff, Ariz., motel room on Aug. 13, 1986. He and [redacted] — also 16 years old then — were on tour of western states with two other boys and a camp counselor when they stopped in Flagstaff for the night on Aug. 12. The western tour is a tradition for campers during their last summer.

Leonard Finz, the Manhattan attorney representing [redacted] and his wife, [redacted] said the camp directors allowed [redacted] to buy the six-inch knife at Yellowstone National Park the day before it was used to stab [redacted] in his sleep.

"This is to punish the camp, its owners and the family for the stabbing of [redacted]" Finz said of the lawsuit.

When [redacted] was discovered, [redacted] had already left, taking the counselor's rental car and $3,000 in travel checks. After eluding police for seven days, [redacted] surrendered, escorted by his parents and attorney.

About a month later, in September 1986, [redacted] telephoned Flagstaff police from a Boston psychiatric center and confessed to murdering [redacted] He was returned to Arizona, where he remains in the Coconino County Jail.

The legal papers say that the [redacted] family—and—the camp owners — the [redacted] family of Princeton, N.J. — had "actual knowledge of the violent, strange, erratic and abnormal behavior exhibited by [redacted] (and) had a duty to warn those to whom [redacted] was entrusted..."

[redacted] mother, is the daughter of [redacted] who own the camp along with other family members.

"There were clear indications that [redacted] should have been under close observation and treatment and not placed with other campers," Finz said.

Prior knowledge of [redacted] psychological problems was revealed during an Arizona hearing earlier this year. It was determined at the hearing that [redacted] was aware of his actions when he stabbed [redacted] and that he should be tried as a adult, despite his age. An appeal is pending.

Finz said that [redacted] who is the son of author [redacted] was known to identify with his father's brother, who is serving a life sentence for his part in a [redacted]

"He [redacted] had a history of violence in school. He was a chronic shoplifter... there is evidence of sexual abuse of his sister," Finz said.

Exactly one year after surrendering to Flagstaff police for the murder of [redacted] — in August 1987 — [redacted] telephoned police and confessed to killing [redacted] She was a University of [redacted] student and part-time waitress, found with her throat slashed and engulfed in flames in her off-campus apartment just before dawn on Oct. 21, 1985.

[redacted] authorities have said they are awaiting the outcome of the Arizona case against [redacted] before making a decision on prosecuting him for [redacted] death.

[redacted] father taught [redacted] studies at the University of [redacted] for 12 years until the family left Laramie for [redacted] about a year ago. He now teaches at the University of [redacted] and recently published two new novels.

A telephone call to him at the university was not returned Tuesday. A message left on an answering machine at an [redacted] telephone listed to [redacted] also went unanswered.

While acknowledging that the $50 million figure was "symbolic," Finz said that a substantial punitive damage award would "punish the wrongdoers while at the same time deterring other camps from such improper actions."

[redacted] said if the lawsuit were successful, part of any money received for the death of his son would be used to enlarge the [redacted] Scholarship Fund at [redacted] and to fund medical research.

"It may sound like an awful amount of money, but when you think of all the pain and suffering we've have been through, the money really isn't the significant thing," he said. "[redacted] was a young man who was always interested in what he could do for others. He wanted to study medicine — to become a doctor."

[redacted]

...killed in August, 1986

The Journal News article describing the tragic events surrounding "Danny's" death.

The Hartford Courant

CLII No. 341 — Thursday, December 7, 1989 — 7 Sections — *7 Copyright 1989

Connecticut news

Jurors find witnesses' duties a thorny issue

Settlement for amputee follows mistrial

By JOANNE JOHNSON
Courant Staff Writer

An out-of-court settlement was reached Wednesday in U.S. District Court in Hartford after a mistrial in a tragic case that focused in part on the obligations of people who witness a person in distress.

James Jandreau, who lost both legs when he was struck by a train in Hartford, contended that his injuries could have been prevented by people who were aware that he was in peril on the tracks.

Jandreau was seeking $17 million in damages.

Jandreau, 28, of Hartford, contended that a security guard who was told of the situation and agreed to help, failed to follow through. Jandreau also said that the man who told the guard of the problem left the area without helping because the guard had said he would handle the situation.

One of Jandreau's attorneys, Leonard L. Finz of New York, said the case could have been "the cutting edge of a new doctrine in Connecticut involving the rescue or aid theory . . . and the theory involving the prevention of aid to someone in distress."

Finz argued that under common law, a person does not have an obligation to come to the aid of a person in distress, but becomes responsible once he or she does undertake that effort.

Finz also argued that Amtrak and Conrail personnel saw Jandreau on the tracks in time to stop the train, but failed to do so.

Defense lawyers argued that the railroad and guard companies were not liable for Jandreau's injuries because he was trespassing and was responsible for his own actions.

Jandreau said that about 7 p.m. on Dec. 23, 1982, he was jogging to his job as a temporary mail handler at the U.S. Post Office on Weston Street. As he climbed a cyclone fence at Union Station to reach an unused section of track that he customarily jogged along on his way to work he slipped, fell and struck his head. Dizzy and disoriented, he wandered into Union Station and back out onto a used section of the track.

John Casale of Plainville, who was sitting in a nearby car, saw Jandreau walk by, say something to a Wells Fargo guard at the station and then walk off. A short time later, Casale saw Jandreau on a train trestle, appearing unsteady and ill. "He was wavering over the railing from the waist back and forth and back and forth. My first concern was that somebody could get hurt," Casale said. Casale testified that he told the security guard, Terrance Chapman, about Jandreau and Chapman said he would take care of the situation.

Chapman said Jandreau appeared unsteady and intoxicated, asking, "Where is the train station?" Chapman said he told Jandreau that the area was not a train station and then Jandreau staggered off.

Chapman testified he told an employee at the Trailways ticket window about Jandreau, but acknowledged that he had not made sure something would be done to help.

Within a few minutes, a three-car train pulling out of the station at 10 or 15 mph struck Jandreau about 380 feet north of the station. Both of his legs were crushed and later amputated. He is confined to a wheelchair.

Jandreau's attorneys contended that Chapman's telling Casale he would take action — but did not — interfered with efforts Casale said he would have made to rescue Jandreau.

Jandreau's lawyers also argued that under common law a person can be found to have committed negligent interference with rescue if he is shown to have interfered with aid efforts that he knew or should have known another person was about to make.

The jury, which listened to testimony for four weeks and deliberated for six days before a mistrial was declared Wednesday, was unable to reach a unanimous decision on whether the accident was Jandreau's fault or the defendants'.

On Monday, four days into deliberations, the jury sent U.S. District Judge T. Emmet Clarie a note saying it had reached a split verdict. The judge asked the jurors to reweigh the evidence carefully in an effort to make a decision.

But Wednesday, just after 11:30 a.m., the jury sent Clarie another note saying it was "irreconcilably deadlocked." The judge declared a mistrial just after 4 p.m. and the agreement was finalized by 5 p.m.

The amount of the settlement for Jandreau was sealed as a term of the agreement. But lawyers for Jandreau said it was sufficient to ensure him financial security in the future.

As Jandreau, a blond-haired, blue-eyed man, left the courthouse, he said, "I feel good. I'm just glad it's over."

The Hartford Courant article describing a major case I tried in the federal court in Hartford, CT.

I am with reporters and TV cameras on a controversial case in New York City. Circa 1990s.

This is a press conference held in my Manhattan office where I am reporting on a high-profile case in the presence of the New York City media.

I am in the conference room of my Manhattan office in front of microphones, reporters, and cameras providing information on a high-profile case I am handling.

I am in my Manhattan office preparing for an ABC-TV interview with Dianne Sawyer.

I am being interviewed by Dianne Sawyer of ABC-TV.

I am in front of the federal courthouse at Foley Square, Manhattan. Photos are being taken for a Newsweek magazine story.on a case of national significance. Circa 1990s.

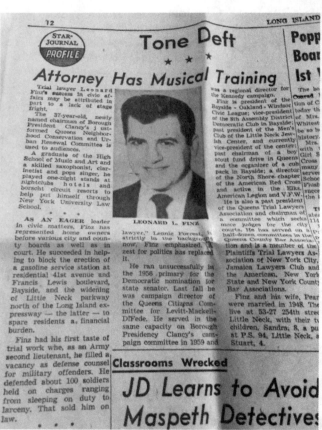

Tone Deft
★ ★ ★
Attorney Has Musical Training

Trial lawyer Leonard Finz's success in civic affairs may be attributed in part to a lack of stage fright.

The 37-year-old, newly named chairman of Borough President Clancy's just-formed Queens Neighborhood Conservation and Urban Renewal Committee is used to audiences.

A graduate of the High School of Music and Art and a skilled saxophonist, clarinetist and pop singer, he played one-night stands at nightclubs hotels and borscht circuit resorts to help put himself through New York University Law School.

★ ★ ★

AS AN EAGER leader in civic matters, Finz has represented home owners before various city and county boards as well as in court. He succeeded in helping to block the erection of a gasoline service station at residential 41st avenue and Francis Lewis boulevard, Bayside, and the widening of Little Neck parkway north of the Long Island expressway — the latter — to spare residents a financial burden.

Finz had his first taste of trial work when, as an Army second lieutenant, he filled a vacancy as defense counsel for military offenders. He defended about 100 soldiers held on charges ranging from sleeping on duty to larceny. That sold him on law.

★ ★ ★

LEONARD L. FINZ

was a regional director for the Kennedy campaign.

Finz is president of the Bayside - Oakland - Windsor Civic League; vice-president of the 8th Assembly District Democratic Club in Bayside; past president of the Men's Club of the Little Neck Jewish Center, and currently vice-president of the center; past chairman of a boy scout fund drive in Queens and the organizer of a cub pack in Bayside; a director of the North Shore chapter of the American Red Cross and active in the Elks, American Legion and V.F.W.

He is also a past president of the Queens Trial Lawyers Association and chairman of a committee which seeks more judges for the city courts. He has served on a half-dozen committees in the Queens County Bar Association and is a member of the Plaintiffs Trial Lawyers Association of New York City, Jamaica Lawyers Club and the American, New York State and New York County Bar Associations.

Finz and his wife, Pearl were married in 1948. They live at 53-27 254th street, Little Neck, with their two children, Sandra, 8, a pupil at P.S. 94, Little Neck, and Stuart, 4.

lawyer," Lennie Forrest, is strictly in the background now, Finz emphasized. A zest for politics has replaced it.

He ran unsuccessfully in the 1956 primary for the Democratic nomination for state senator. Last fall he was campaign director of the Queens Citizens Committee for Levitt-Mackell-DiFede. He served in the same capacity on Borough Presidency Clancy's campaign committee in 1959 and

Classrooms Wrecked

JD Learns to Avoid Maspeth Detectives

An article published in the Long Island Press.

Media coverage on a case making the news. Circa 1990s.

During a press conference on a case of significance. Circa 1990s.

I am holding a press conference in my office. The photo in the background is of New York State Supreme Court Justices. I am somewhere in that group. Circa 1990s.

Getting the mic set in place for a TV interview held in my office.

Boy given 3M in suit

Seriously hurt by car in '83

By BILL FARRELL
Daily News Staff Writer

A 16-year-old boy, seriously injured when he was struck by a car, was awarded $3 million in an out-of-court settlement only moments before the opening arguments were about to be heard in Brooklyn Supreme Court yesterday.

The case stemmed from a January 1983 accident in which Velimir Andric, formerly of Greenpoint, was struck by an uninsured car owned and operated by Denise Gambella. Velimir, who was returning from school, suffered several broken bones and some internal damage.

The boy's lawyer, Leonard Finz, said the child received the large award because Gambella, employed by Deven Lithographers Inc., of Greenpoint, had been sent to buy coffee for co-workers when her car hit the boy.

Finz argued that since the car was not insured and Gambella was working—by going to get coffee—at the time of the accident, the Deven firm also should be held responsible.

Velimir, whose family moved from Brooklyn to upstate Monticello, where they run small summer cottages, will receive large lump-sum payments, start-

'He is assured not only a fine education, but he will also be able to provide a solid education for his children.'

Lawyer
Leonard Finz

ing on his 18th birthday, to pay for his education. He will also receive large lump-sum payments on his 21st, 25th, and 30th birthdays, and every five years thereafter.

The smiling youngster just shrugged his shoulders when asked how he felt about the amount of money

DAILY NEWS   Friday, March 28, 1986

$3 MILLION SMILES adorn faces of Velimir Andric, lawyer Leonard Finz and Velimir's dad, Milenio (standing)

NICK SORRENTINO/DAILY NEWS

he'll be receiving. Finz, however, said the boy will have a steady monthly in-   come for the rest of his life.
"He is assured not only a fine education, but he will   also be able to provide a solid education for his children."

The Daily News story of my young client struck by a car owned by an employee who was sent out by her employer to get coffee from a nearby diner.

The injured boy with his arm around me. His father and the Brooklyn Supreme Court is in the background. A Daily News press photo.

I am describing to the press how a fire in a large high-rise garbage chute took the lives of several tenants at Shomberg Plaza, New York City. Circa 1990s.

A one-on-one TV interview. Circa 1990s.

I am making a point in front of news cameras. Circa 1980s.

I am ready for a one-on-one interview with Bill O'Reilly's "Inside Edition" aired on NBC-TV. Circa 1990s.

Thursday, June 1, 1995

$2.7 Million Accord In Aerosol-Fire Suit

A $2.75 million settlement has been reached in a action brought by two women who were burned after an aerosol insecticide ignited and caused a flash fire in a kitchen.

The plaintiffs, Anne Johnson and Julia Kono, claimed the defective design of the can permitted the insecticide to ignite from a pilot light on a stove. Earlier in the litigation, claims tied to the product's failure to contain adequate warnings were dismissed in Brooklyn Supreme Court on federal preemption grounds because the Environmental Protection Agency had approved the can's labeling.

The plaintiffs were represented by Leonard L. Finz, Stuart L. Finz and Joseph Lichtenstein of Finz & Finz; Johnson Chemical Co., the distributor of the product, by Warren Sanger of Bower, Sanger & Futterman; Aerofil, the manufacturer, by Dudley Thompson of Ayers & Thompson; J.L. Variety, the retailer, by Peter Ledwith of White Quinlan Staley & Ledwith of Garden City, L.I. The settlement was reached last week as a trial was to begin before Brooklyn Supreme Court Justice Melvin Barasch.

A New York Law Journal story describing an insecticide that exploded and seriously injured my clients. Circa 1980s.

NEW YORK POST

TUESDAY, OCTOBER 19, 1982   30 CENTS   © 1982 News Group Publications Inc. Vol. 181, No. 289
AMERICA'S FASTEST-GROWING NEWSPAPER

Woman wins $3M in crash helmet suit

By AL SOSTCHEN

A JURY in Bronx Supreme Court awarded $3 million yesterday to a prospective bride who was injured in a motorcycle accident because her crash helmet failed to provide proper protection.

In a coma for seven weeks after the accident in August, 1977, Denise Cornier suffered permanent brain damage. Her marriage was called off.

According to her attorney, Leonard Finz, the same model helmet had failed an impact test conducted by the U.S. Dept. of Transportation nine months before the accident.

Finz said his client suffered "severe brain damage" and was currently undergoing treatment in the NYU Medical Center head trauma program for double vision, loss of memory and lack of coordination.

He said his client was riding on a motorcycle operated by James Spagna, then her fiance, when the cycle collided with a car. Miss Cornier, now 28, was hurled through the air and sustained severe brain damage.

Finz said the same type of helmet had failed the U.S. tests in 1976.

Spagna had purchased the helmet from a Manhattan dealership in May, 1977, three months before the accident.

Finz said the Bell Helmet Corp., of Norwalk, Cal. discontinued the model after the accident.

The award was against Bell, Spagna, and Mack Davis, the operator of the second vehicle.

The press article in the New York Post describing the Bell Helmet verdict. Circa 1980s.

New York Law Journal

Thursday, May 16, 1985

Injured Stagehand Gets Settlement of $5 Million

A structured settlement valued at $5 million was reached this week on behalf of a former stagehand who fell thirty-five feet from a chair at a Broadway theatre while repairing a spotlight and suffered a severe spinal cord injury.

The settlement took place during a trial this week in State Supreme Court in Manhattan in the matter by Robert E. Foster Jr. against the ANTA Theatre and the producers of "Bubbling Brown Sugar," the musical that was playing at the time of the accident in November, 1977.

According to Leonard L. Finz, who represented the plaintiff along with Bradley A. Sacks, the settlement calls for the waiver of a Workers' Compensation lien of nearly $500,000, a cash payment of $4,000,000 monthly payments of $4,000 for life and supplements; cash payments every four years for twenty-eight years. The theatre was represented by Eugene McGarry of O'Brien, McGarry, Murph & Mayr of Rockville Centre, L.I.; the producers by Warren Sanger of Bower & Gardner.

Photo courtesy of N.Y. News (not part of New York Law Journal article)

Leonard L. Finz, Robert E. Foster, Bradley A. Sacks

A tragic case in which my client's feet were severed, and a microsurgical miracle performed by doctor's. 1985.

DAILY NEWS

NEW YORK'S PICTURE NEWSPAPER

Loses right foot, left leg under train

By DON GENTILE

A 19-year-old girl's left leg was severed and she lost her right foot yesterday when she fell beneath a Conrail train as it left a Harlem-bound train on its way upstate.

The train crew apparently was unaware that the girl had been struck and the diesel train continued on its way to Poughkeepsie, a Conrail spokesman said.

The girl, Adrienne Brown of 1454 Walton ave. Bronx, was taken to Bellevue Hospital where doctors from the now-famous microsurgery team headed by reattached her left foot and leg. The surgery was completed at 9:15 p.m. after eight hours, and Brown "tolerated the procedure very well," a hospital spokesman said.

Hospital officials said the girl's right leg, which was severed below the knee was beyond repair and it was decided to attempt the unusual procedure in order to provide her with at least a partial support for her body.

The officials explained that if the operation worked but if the foot could be surgically removed.

Paramedics Miguel Cruz and Joyce Ravis who brought Brown to Bellevue said the girl who remained conscious told them she had been talking along the edge of the platform as the train was pulling out of the station.

"First to come to Brown's aid was Transit Police Officer Terrence Fischman who was on duty in the station along with his partner John Gentile.

"She was lying on her stomach and she was conscious. Fischman said. She said she thought her legs were broken and said 'Just let me get up. I'll be all right.'"

But Fischman could see that the train had crushed the right foot and severed the left leg below the knee.

Gentile ran to a nearby firehouse, returned with a bed sheet and placed the ankles around the injured limbs.

The paramedics immobilized both legs with an air splint and rushed Bellevue to have its microsurgery team on standby. A police escort cleared a route for the ambulance through city streets and down the FDR Drive.

The Conrail spokesman said they would conduct a thorough questioning of the train crew.

The train had come to a stop and the accident happened as the train was leaving the station. She apparently fell between the third and the last FDR, the wheels of that car running over her, the spokesman said. "The crew's check the platform before they signal for the train to move out."

THE RESULT
April 25, 1985

Awarded 5M in train mishap

A Queens woman yesterday won a $5 million settlement for a 1979 Metro North train accident in which she lost her right foot and left leg when she fell under a train at Harlem's 125th St. and Park ave. station.

Bellevue Hospital surgeons were able to reattach the severed left foot of Adrienne Brown, 26, to her right leg in the first micro-surgical lower transposition performed in the United States. Her attorney, Leonard Finz, a former judge, and Richard O'Keeffe, counsel for the Metropolitan Transportation Authority, agreed to the out-of-court settlement minutes before jury selection. Under the agreement Brown will receive tax-free payments plus interest over a 30-year period.

—Bernard Rabin

Police administer first aid to 19-year-old Adrienne Brown as she lies on tracks at Conrail's 125th St. station. Brown had been walking along the edge of the above-ground platform as a train was pulling out. She lost her balance, fell against the train and finally beneath the last car.

The news story of my client who was tragically injured while working as a Broadway musical stagehand. 1985.

An Award of Honor presented to me as the "Man of the Year." 1979.

The New York Times

NEW YORK, FRIDAY, SEPTEMBER 9, 1988

Let Congress Do Justice on Military Contractors

To the Editor

A basic irony is emerging in our Government's approach to compensating victims of its mistakes. On the one hand, controversy surrounds the granting of financial awards to the families of the victims of Iran Air Flight 655, shot down by a United States Navy guided missile over the Persian Gulf, resulting in the loss of 290 lives. On the other, the Supreme Court has held 5 to 4 in Boyle v. United Technologies Corporation that the manufacturer of a helicopter built in accordance with Government specifications would not be required to compensate the family of a Navy pilot who drowned when his craft plunged into the ocean, trapping him underwater as he tried unsuccessfully to push open an escape hatch.

Both situations raise serious questions of fundamental justice and the separation of power. The Iran tragedy is interwoven in the politics of international conflict and expediency, which may result in payment to the victims' survivors to impress the world with our basic sense of justice. Whether this is acceptable depends upon one's philosophical and humanitarian beliefs. At the same time, the death of Lieut. David Boyle is intertwined in a judicial decision that appears to "legislate" a favored place within our society for major defense contractors, with a resulting denial to the victim's survivors. Because of one's deep philosophical and humanitarian beliefs however, this result is not acceptable.

Lieutenant Boyle's family sued United Technologies Corporation (Sikorsky), charging that the design of the escape hatch of the helicopter he was flying was defective and caused his death. A Federal jury in Virginia agreed and awarded his estate $725,000. The verdict, however, was set aside and the suit dismissed by the United States Court of Appeals for the Fourth Circuit. The Circuit Court relied on the "military contractor defense," which in essence immunizes the manufacturer, who worked from Government-supplied specifications. The Supreme Court, while expressing confusion about the Circuit Court's dismissal, in effect, made the "military contractor defense" the

law of the land. In support of the decision, Associate Justice Antonin Scalia wrote, "The financial burden of judgments against the contractors would ultimately be passed through, substantially if not totally, to the United States itself."

In a sharp dissent, Justice William J. Brennan Jr., joined by Justices Thurgood Marshall and Harry A. Blackmun, was most critical of the majority's judicial usurpation of the legislative role. "Were I a legislator," Justice Brennan wrote: "I would probably vote against any law absolving multimillion-dollar private enterprises from answering for their tragic mistakes, at least if that law were justified by no more than the unsupported speculation that their liability might ultimately burden the United States Treasury. Some of my colleagues here would evidently vote otherwise (as they have here), but that should not matter here. We are judges not legislators, and the vote is not ours to cast."

Both the Boyle case and Tozer v. LTV Corp. (decided the same day) confer a gift of exculpation on the wrongdoer, while removing a basic right, thereby placing an overwhelming burden on the victim and the victim's family. As Justice Brennan said: "In my view, this Court lacks both authority and expertise to fashion such a rule, whether to protect the Treasury of the United States or the coffers of industry."

In a separate dissent, Justice John Paul Stevens wrote, "When judges are asked to embark on a lawmaking venture, I believe they should carefully consider whether they, or a legislative body, are better equipped to perform the task at hand."

As to the Iran tragedy — where the principles of fundamental justice take us is for public opinion ultimately to decide. But as to the hundreds of Lieutenant Boyles and their families who will fall victim to the negligence of military contractors in the future, it seems clear Congress must act to correct the inequity created by our highest Court. Not only would such action fall properly within the Constitutional domain, but it would also be unquestionably the clearest evidence of fundamental justice at work!

LEONARD L. FINZ
New York, Aug. 22, 1988

The writer is a former justice of the New York State Supreme Court.

My letter to the New York Times calling for "fundamental justice." 1988.

A Proclamation from the United States Congress presented to me by Honorable Gary L Ackermann, Member of Congress, for distinguished service to the community.

The Leadership Award presented to me as chairman of the Queens Lawyers Division, Federation of Jewish Philanthropies.

The certificate awarded to me as a faculty member of the National Judicial College, University of Nevada, Reno. 1977.

The late Chief Justice of The Supreme Court, Warren E. Burger, presenting me with the five year faculty award from New York Law School for my service as a professor of law. 1985.

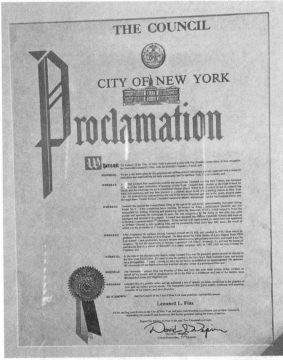

The Proclamation from the New York City Council that was presented to me by Councilman David L. Weprin, for distinguished service. 2008.

The Citation from Nassau County Executive Thomas R. Suozzi, for "selfless commitment to the community." 2008.

I am holding a press conference with local TV channels on an important case of community interest. Circa 1980s.

AS PUBLISHED IN

The New York Jury Verdict Reporter

XVIII/21-53 SNOW-TUBING ACCIDENT — HILL DESIGN — BRAIN DAMAGE AND BLINDNESS IN ONE EYE

SETTLEMENT: Devora Tilson, as g.a.l. of Jack Tilson v. State of New York Claim No. 96213 Date of Settlement 3/24/00 Court of Claims

Pltf. Atty: Leonard L. Finz, Stuart L. Finz, and Jay L. Feigenbaum of Finz & Finz, Jericho

The settlement with New York State in the sum of $8 million, regarding a snow tubing accident. It was reported as the highest tort settlement against the state at the time. 2000.

Clmts. settled for a total of $8,000,000 in this case ($5,000,000 for Jack T. and $3,000,000 for Devora T.), which arose out of an accident that occurred on 2/9/97 when Clmt. Jack Tilson, a 52-year-old real estate developer and builder, was injured while using a snow tube at Belleayre Mountain Ski Center. In a prior decision on 10/15/98, the court granted Clmts.' motion for summary judgment on-liability, finding that the slope of the hill on which Clmt. was tubing was negligently designed and constructed for the planned activity, in that the snow tube trail did not have a straight, level area where the tubes and their riders could slow down and come to a complete stop. The court found that the hill was designed with a 90° turn at the bottom, and the berm at the bottom of the hill was inadequate to prevent the tubes from leaving the course. As Clmt. descended the hill in his snow tube, he vaulted over the berm and left the course, continuing down the embankment where he crashed into a tree.

Deft. had argued that Clmt. assumed the risk of the sport. The court rejected this defense based upon the fact that the risk of leaving the trail was not readily apparent and was not a foreseeable risk of the activity.

Injuries: depressed skull fracture with cranio-cerebral trauma, resulting in severe brain damage with cognitive impairments, trauma-induced dementia, and memory loss; blindness in one eye; fractured facial bones. Clmt. underwent multiple surgeries and has developed seizures. Clmt. contended that he requires constant care and is no longer employable. ⋈

A press conference, while at the same time being interviewed via the telephone on live radio. Circa 1980s. The photo on the left was published in the New York press.

A photo of Luis Lajara Homero Burgos (in the circle) being honored in Spain prior to his being wrongfully charged with shoplifting at Alexander's department store.

The New York Times

NEW YORK, SATURDAY, JANUARY 19, 1985

Dominican Wins $1 Million Award

By United Press International

A political leader from the Dominican Republic was awarded $1 million yesterday in a suit that charged Alexander's Department Store with falsely accusing him and his wife of shoplifting in 1976.

The man — Luis Homero Lajára Burgos, leader of the Partido Demócrata Popular and a 1974 opponent of President Joaquín Balaguer — was awarded $100,000 actual damages and $900,000 punitive damages by a State Supreme Court jury in Manhattan.

Mr. Burgos said in the suit that publicity from the incident cost him votes in the 1978 Dominican national election.

The New York Times article describing the Burgos verdict against Alexander's department store.

Here, I am answering questions posed by reporters on a current New York City case at the time.

I am at home in my study working on a legal brief.

The New York Times

Copyright © 1986 The New York Times   NEW YORK, THURSDAY, DECEMBER 25, 1986

Column One

The Law

Deadline

With five months gone and only seven to go, lawyers are worried that many potential litigants have not yet heard that they can bring certain lawsuits that would otherwise be barred because of the passage of time. These people are victims of the latent effects of exposure to five toxic substances: DES or diethylstilbestrol; asbestos; tungsten carbide; chlordane, and PVC, or polyvinylchloride.

The State Legislature passed a law last July that gave those victims one year in which to revive their legal claims by filing lawsuits. The year ends next July 29.

The president of the State Trial Lawyers Association, Perry Pazer, and one of the state's leading products-liability lawyers, Leonard L. Finz, have been spreading the word through lectures to lawyers and environmentalists, among others. Mr. Finz has also appeared on talk shows and used the publicity surrounding the filing of a DES case to get the word out.

The lawyers said that what began as a trickle of telephone inquiries has recently begun to pick up, indicating that the message may be reaching beyond the state's lawyers and legislators.

The statement printed by The New York Times describing me as, "one of the state's leading products-liability lawyers. 1986.

Jury Awards $5 Million In Truck Driver's Death

A Brooklyn jury has awarded $5 million to the family of a truck driver who was killed in a 1976 collision with a bus on the New Jersey Turnpike. According to counsel in the case, the verdict for wrongful death of Henry R. Purdie could approach $6.5 million with the addition of interest. Evidence at the trial, which ended late Wednesday, showed that the Mr. Purdie, thirty years old at the time, was killed when a repair van in which he was riding was struck by a Trailways bus and forced off the highway into a tree.

The decedent, a Brooklyn resident, had summoned the repair van after his truck became disabled on the Turnpike. He was riding in that vehicle behind a truck towing his disabled truck. Justice Gerald S. Held, who presided at the ten-day trial, yesterday rejected a motion to dismiss the award on the basis of excessiveness. The estate, a wife and three children, was represented by Leonard L. Finz of Julien, Schlesinger & Finz; the defendant owner of the bus, Continental Southeastern Lines, by Harold Berel of Berel, Navarro & Mullen.

A New York Law Journal article describing a verdict received on behalf of my client in the Brooklyn Supreme Court. 1981.

DAILY NEWS

30¢   NEW YORK, FRIDAY, JANUARY 28, 1983   Chance of flurri

$4.5M malpractice award

Nearly $4.5 million has been awarded to the wife and daughters of a 33-year-old Rockland County man who died of a heart attack soon after his chest pains were diagnosed as a digestive disorder.

The award, believed the largest in Rockland County history, was set Wednesday night by a six-member jury, who found ███████████ of New City guilty of malpractice. The award was presented to ██████████ of New City, the wife of Martin ████████ who died in 1973 after experiencing chest pains. Zemek had diagnosed Morgenroth's condition as a hiatus hernia—a hernia on the esophagus.

—Mary Ann Giordano

A Daily News article describing a verdict received on behalf of my client in Rockland County, New York. 1983.

Estate Gets $2.6 Million In Wrong-Diagnosis Suit

A Rockland County jury awarded $2,670,000 Wednesday to the estate of a thirty-three-year-old man who died from a heart condition five days after his doctor had diagnosed his complaint of chest pains as a gastrointestinal disorder. With interest dating back to the 1973, the date of death, the award will total approximately $4.4 million, reportedly one of the largest ever in the county. The award was returned in favor of Rochelle Morgenroth, as administrix of the estate of her husband, Martin, who had been an electro-plater in a metals firm. The verdict was against Dr. Lionel Zemek of New City. The plaintiff was represented by Leonard H. Finz and Bradley A. Sacks of Julien Schlesinger & Finz; the defendant by Kingdon T. Locker of Clark, Gagliardi & Miller of White Plains. Rockland Surrogate John Skahen, sitting by designation, presided over the trial in State Supreme Court.

The New York Law Journal article describing the "wrong-diagnosis suit."

New York Governor Mario Cuomo congratulating me as being named "Man of the Year" by the Federation of Jewish Philanthropies.

New York State Governor Mario Cuomo presents me with a "Man of the Year" award. Looking on is the Dean of the National Judicial College.

Profile Of

Hon. Leonard L. Finz

by Lester Shick*

What was written to describe former Supreme Court Justice Leonard L. Finz at a dinner held by the UJA/Federation of Jewish Philanthropies honoring him as "Man of the Year" is an accurate summary of his deeds and accomplishments.

"A superb, tireless, selfless worker for countless charities, religious, fraternal and professional causes, and possessed with a rare gift for humanity, Judge Finz has always been the leader. Elected at age 39 as a Civil Court Judge, his profound sense of justice and commitment to academic excellence merited his promotion to Justice of the Supreme Court. A prolific author, his many innovative, far reaching, and landmark opinions and articles, have been published, widely cited, and have carved new frontiers in the law.

The founder of the Brandeis Association, its Chairman of the Board for seven years, and the appointment for life as its Honorary Chairman of the Board, are but few of the many splendid honors he has received. A professor of law, a nationally known lecturer, a faculty member of the National Judicial College, he served also as the only Queens representative on the Mayor's Committee on the Judiciary for six years, by appointment of the then Presiding Justice of the Appellate Division, Second Department.

We, his colleagues and friends, pay tribute to this former premier Judge–now a premier trial lawyer, and bestow our highest award to Judge Leonard L. Finz - a premier human being!"

Those words were written after Judge Finz resigned from the Supreme Court to become a partner to the late Al Julien, one of the national superstars of the tort Bar. Within a short time, Lenny Finz was scoring record high verdicts throughout the state. He also won the very first DES case in the nation based upon the novel theory of concert of action. The verdict in *Bichler v. Eli Lily* is the landmark DES case that reached the US Supreme Court, and is recognized as one of the leading cases in the nation on drug products liability. The *Bichler* verdict also opened the door for thousands of DES victims who had previously been shut out.

Born on the lower East side, his natural gift for music showed itself early on with a unique talent for singing. At age 9, his parents, despite hard times and the Depression, bought him a saxophone, paying $1.00 a week, and starting him with weekly music lessons at 50 cents. Then living in Brooklyn, he was accepted as a gifted music student to the High School of Music and Art in upper

Hon. Leonard L. Finz

Manhattan, where he traveled four hours a day on subways to and from school. An already accomplished musician, he played first clarinet in the Music and Art Symphony Orchestra, and was the leader of the school's jazz band.

Following graduation, Lenny entered NYU as a pre-med student. But midway into the first semester, he was drafted into the US Army as part of the first 18 year old draft of WWII, and had to withdraw from school. After completing basic training, Lenny's talent was soon discovered and he was appointed by Special Services as Camp Entertainment Director, where he wrote, performed, directed and produced army shows for the entertainment of the thousands of GI's on the base. The widely circulated army newspaper carried his picture and bio entitled, "Pvt. Lenny Finz - Born of Talent."

Wanting to be a part of the war, he applied to, and was accepted in, Officer's Candidate School, where after four months of intense training he graduated a Second Lieutenant in the Field Artillery.

Within a short time, Lenny was trained in Japanese to become part of the assault forces in the invasion of Japan. He was on a troop ship in the Pacific when the atomic bomb was dropped and Japan surrendered. The ship continued onto Leyte in the Philippines where he was then asked to serve as Defense Counsel in army courts-martial cases. Although only a high school graduate, he learned the drill, and defended almost 100 GI's charged with varying crimes. As a result of his efforts, he received a commendation, and was promoted to First Lieutenant for his outstanding service.

After 43 months in the service, he entered NYU where he completed college, and then went onto NYU Law, earning two degrees in five years. Throughout college and law school, he earned his way playing in bands at weddings often performing in such Catskill resorts as Grossingers, the Concord and Browns. It was after graduating from NYU Law and while entertaining at Grossingers that an agent from MCA - the then largest theatrical agency in the world, contacted, and signed him to a two year contract with MCA. "I gave myself two years to make it in show business - if it didn't happen, I would return to law." It was then that he, and Steve Lawrence, also handled by MCA, were chosen by Billboard and Cashbox magazines as the "male singing stars" of the future. While Steve Lawrence made it big in show business, Lenny came close, playing nite clubs all over the country and doing a weekly TV show on ABC-TV. Having met, and encouraged by Al Jolson who saw him perform, he later was featured at the Jolson Memorial held at Madison Square Garden before 18,000 people where he sang a medley of Jolson songs in honor of the old master. Lenny also auditioned for the movie, *The Jazz Singer*, and was a serious contender to Danny Thomas who was ultimately selected for the role. Coming close was not enough and after two years he started his own law practice.

Moving into an office on Jamaica Avenue which he shared with two old time Jamaica lawyers, he leaned toward personal injury work. Within a short time he was a regular plaintiff's trial lawyer, appearing in Civil Court almost everyday. He also received the first $10,000.00 verdict in the Civil Court, which at that time was the Court's top jurisdiction and for 1962 was quite an accomplishment.

Lenny's show business background was soon recognized when he was called upon by the Queens Democratic Organization to plan political rallies for statewide and national campaigns. It was in 1960, when President John F. Kennedy, then a candidate for President, came to Queens and Lenny was assigned the task of organizing the giant rally to be held at Sunnyside Gardens for JFK. "President Kennedy was running three hours late and the then DA Frank O'Connor and I, had to hold the crowds until Kennedy arrived. "Introducing the future President of the United States to the thousands of people in the audience, is something I will never forget."

Winning a primary for Civil Court, he became a Civil Court Judge in 1966 where he amassed one of the highest settlement records in the State. In 1974 he was elected to the Supreme Court.

(Continued on page 18)

Profile Of: Hon. Leonard Finz *(continued from page 3)*

ing met, and encouraged by Al Jolson who saw him perform, he later was featured at the Jolson Memorial held at Madison Square Garden before 18,000 people where he sang a medley of Jolson songs in honor of the old master. Lenny also auditioned for the movie, *The Jazz Singer*, and was a serious contender to Danny Thomas who was ultimately selected for the role. Coming close was not enough and after two years he started his own law practice.

As a Judge, he had many published opinions, many of which became feature articles on the front page of the NY Law Journal. His listing in Martindale-Hubbel, with its highest rating for ability and ethics, also enumerates the many articles published, awards received, and other high accomplishments. He was also the innovator of the high-lo contract which is in wide use nationally.

Today, Judge Finz is senior partner of the firm he founded 13 years ago, and is known as Finz & Finz. The firm, which is managed by his partner and son, Stuart, is always on the search for new and cutting-edge litigation. Recently, his firm has mounted an assault against the tobacco industry.

Whimsically, Lenny Finz says, "In my next life I want to come back as a director and producer of motion pictures or theatrical productions. And if there is life after that, I can then decide which was more fulfilling, law or show business." "But then again," he muses, "being a trial lawyer really combines both worlds, which makes me a very fortunate and grateful person indeed."

He is also grateful that he has been married to Pearl, his wife of almost 49 years, with two children, Saundra, a nurse with two degrees and his lawyer son Stuart. Both are married to lawyers and each has two children giving Pearl and Lenny four grandchildren in all. "Tennis keeps my body agile, my grandchildren keep my energy high, and the law keeps my mind active. Hey, I'm a lucky guy, and will go with all three just as long as I can."

*Editor's Note: Lester Shick, a Senior Court Clerk, is a frequent contributor to the Queens Bar Bulletin. He gratefully acknowledges the assistance of Mitchell Caspert in the preparation of this article.

A profile appearing in the Queens Bar Bulletin. 1997.

An explosive novel I authored (and was published), describing a "Divided America."

A novel I authored (and was published), dealing with, "Corruption, Love, Indian casino gambling, and the Mob."

A photo used on the back cover of one of my published novels as the author. 2006.

A thriller novel I authored (and was published), of "Corruption, Love and Tragedy."

Finz' next chapter to storied career

BY BILL
SAN ANTONIO

Depending on what decade you were in, you may have encountered Leonard Finz on a beach in the South Pacific, on-stage in a smoky nightclub, presiding over a courtroom in New York City or on the cover of a pulpy paperback.

The soon-to-be 89-year-old, who has lived in the Village of North Hills' Gracewood community for the last 15-odd years, has lived a life that has seen its share of unexpected turns as a soldier-turned-jazz singer-turned-lawyer-turned state Supreme Court Justice, but each has led to his current professional undertaking, that of a novelist.

Finz' latest book, a thriller called "Reservation to Kill," released last week by Roundtree Mysteries Inc., follows Justice Department agent Matt Connors as he investigates the murder of a top ranking federal officer and in the process unravels a shady plot to build an Indian casino in the Catskill Mountains.

"As a trial lawyer, it's important to tell a story to a jury so they could get the essence and depth and meaning and emo-

Leonard Finz used his experiences as a soldier, entertainer and state Supreme Court justice in writing his three novels.

tion of a human issue, and that's what I try to do in my writing," he said at his home Saturday.

Finz grew up in Bensonhurst, Brooklyn and entered New York University's pre-med program in 1942, but midway through his first semester he was drafted into World War II and left school having earned no college credit.

Finz grew up playing the clarinet and saxophone, and after entering the army in 1943 he began performing shows on his base that caught the eye of the military's bandleader.

"He said, 'Lenny, I've got to get you in,'" Finz said.

The gigs were steady but unrewarding, he said, as those he entertained were the ones seeing action on the front lines.

"I didn't want to have to tell my future children and future grandchildren that I spent my time playing the clarinet on play grounds while others were sacrificing themselves on the beaches of an attack in the pacific," Finz said.

In an effort to get closer to the fight, Finz applied for Officer's Candidate School in a move that may have seemed a bit facetious at the time.

Continued on Page 44

Finz leaps from bench to pulp novels

Continued from Page 3

Finz had only achieved the rank of a first-class private, and entered the highly competitive Field Artillery School in Port Sill, Okla. for an intensive four-month training program during which candidates were cut and released each week.

One hundred enrolled at the start of class, Finz said. Thirty-two graduated on May 5, 1945.

Finz was among them.

"I knew full well that when I applied for Officer Candidate School that I'd be going overseas and getting into battle," Finz said. "I knew that and I wanted that."

Now a 2nd lieutenant specializing in artillery in the U.S. Army, Finz was sent to California for training in Japanese language and customs, weaponry and military strategy, participating in daily beach assault runs.

Assigned to Okinawa, Japan as part of the 27th Division overseeing the first wave of an attack, Finz was in the Pacific for 32 days when he learned the United States had dropped atomic bombs on Hiroshima and Nagasaki and that the Japanese had surrendered.

Finz was re-routed to the Philippine island of Leyte and tasked with repatriating Filipinos who had been driven from their homes during the war by the Japanese.

After a number of months on the job, Finz was called upon by his commanding officer for a somewhat unconventional assignment.

"He called me into his office and said, 'Finz, I would like you to accept an assignment, and I want you to know that you do not have to accept it, but I would like you to,'" Finz said. "He went on to say that there were hundreds of G.I.s that were rotting in our guard houses and jails and

that he had to gather a court marshaled board to handle these trials. There was only one lawyer on the island, but he had to serve as the prosecutor, and according to the Court Marshal's Manual, defense counsel had to be an officer."

At the time, Finz had only a high school education, but accepted the task and began reading legal manuals to learn the procedural process, traveling into the jungles at night to gather witnesses and evidence to use in court.

"It was a dangerous assignment because some of the Japanese were still hiding out in caves, either not knowing the war was over or not wanting to admit they lost," Finz said.

Finz tried the cases and earned 1st lieutenant honors before his discharge in August of 1946, and met his soon-to-be wife Pearl while on terminal leave from the service.

When Finz returned from the war, he enrolled again at NYU on the G.I. Bill majoring in history and English, later graduating from law school and passing the New York state bar examination in 1951. He also joined the local Associated Musicians of Greater New York, joining a band that sought a saxophone player who could sing.

"I figured I'd try this out for two years and if I make it I'll stick with it," Finz said.

Before long, Finz was playing five club nights a week and attracting the likes of Al Jolson, who saw him perform at a Milwaukee lounge in 1949 and complimented his style after the show.

"I had a big belting kind of voice," Finz said. "I was compared to Al Jolson, not that I played his kind of music but I was that kind of performer."

Finz was later invited to sing at the Al Jolson memorial concert at Madison

Square Garden after the singer's death in 1950, and Billboard Magazine referred to Lennie Forrest and Steve Lawrence, a contemporary, as "Singers of the Future," Finz said, and he even came close to landing the lead role in the 1952 version of "The Jazz Singer," which went to Danny Thomas.

"You've got to remember, Danny Thomas was a big name at the time," Finz said. "Lenny Forrest, I was just getting started."

By the late 1950s, Finz had abandoned music and gone on to practice law, and his prestige rose such that he ran for Congress in 1962 and became President John F. Kennedy's spokesman in Queens and Nassau on Medicare, which would later be passed under President Lyndon B. Johnson.

In 1965, Finz was elected as a judge to the New York City Civil court, and would later be elected a state Supreme Court Justice, where he would serve until 1978 before stepping down to practice as a trial lawyer.

"It was unheard of that a young judge would resign from the state Supreme Court," Finz said.

Finz said he considers his landmark case to be a successful 1979 lawsuit against the pharmaceutical manufacturer Eli Lily and Company, whose medication to curb miscarriages resulted in daughters born to those patients to have vaginal cancer.

To reach a favorable verdict, Finz had to specifically link Lily to the vaginal cancers springing up, a difficult task because of the variety of copycat drugs on the market at the time.

But Finz argued on a theory that if Lily hadn't initially put its drug, known as Diethylstilbestrol, on the market, the

copycats would not have existed.

"It opened the gates of justice for other victims to go ahead with their own proceedings," Finz said.

In 1984, Finz founded the medical malpractice firm Finz & Finz, P.C., which has offices in Mineola and Manhattan and is currently operated by Finz's son Stuart.

The Finz family may soon be able to operate as its own firm, as Stuart's wife Cheri is a lawyer, their daughter Jacqueline recently graduated from Toro Law School and is studying for the bar exam, and their son Brandon graduated from the University of Miami School of Business and will attend Georgetown University's law school this fall.

Leonard Finz' daughter Saundra is married to Jerrold Parker, a founding partner of the medical malpractice firm Parker Waichman LLP, whose Long Island office is based in Port Washington. Their daughter Brittany is set to graduate from the University of Baltimore's School of Law, and their son Sean will enter Loyola University New Orleans College of Law this fall.

"To think, it all started in 1945 when I was assigned as a defense counsel as a high school graduate," Finz said.

Finz said he draws upon his life experiences as a soldier, entertainer and judge to come up with the "plenty of ideas" he has for future novels, hoping to build upon a possible Connors series following two unrelated works, "Arrowhead" (2005) and "The Paragon Conspiracy" (2011).

"I'm hoping someone is at the other end of my words and being moved by what I have to say and what I have to write about," Finz said.

He added, "If the good lord is amenable, I hope to write a dozen more."

An article describing my role as a published author of thriller novels. 2013.

ABOUT MY FAMILY

What follows is a brief segment on my family in keeping with the spirit of this memoir...

Pearl and I had a wonderful marriage for 67 ½ years. She was my best friend and passed away in May, 2016. A college graduate, she majored in Philosophy where such names as Socrates, Plato, and Aristotle, were almost members of our family. She was also extraordinarily talented as a most creative interior decorator. Fashion, charm, personality, and love of family were her constant companions.

My daughter, Saundra Parker, is a retired Registered Nurse with two degrees, one from Hofstra University, the other from the State University of New York at Stony Brook. Receiving many commendations from the Long Island Jewish Hospital where she was a Special Nurse on the "Head and Neck" floor, she joined up with Dr. Alex Keller, a renowned breast reconstruction and cosmetic surgeon of New York. (She was accepted to medical school, but opted for a nursing career instead.)

Saundra, who we call Sandy, is married to Jerry Parker, a peer reviewed and nationally reputed lawyer who received his college degree (B.A.) from Queens College in New York City and law degree (JD) from St. John's University Law School. A former federal treasury agent, he is a highly-recognized specialist and expert in mass tort litigation and an acknowledged national champion on behalf of consumers of dangerous drugs in his many successful challenges against the pharmaceutical industry. The senior partner of Parker and Waichman LLP, the firm represents clients in a multitude of high-level cases throughout the country.

My son Stuart Finz is the CEO of Finz & Finz, a national law firm, and a premier trial attorney. He is a graduate of C.W. Post College in New York (B.A.) and has a law degree (JD) from the Thomas Jefferson School of Law, San Diego, California. He received a record $20.5 million verdict in New York State on behalf of a lung cancer victim against the giant cigarette maker Phillip Morris, and a record $24.5 million settlement in a truck accident case. His many multi-million dollar verdicts and settlements have also accounted for his being specially selected and peer reviewed as a member of "Super Lawyers", "Million Dollar Advocates Forum", "New York

Law Journal Report of Largest Verdicts", and others.

Cheri Einbinder Finz, Stuart's wife, is also an attorney, having earned a B.A. at the University of Maryland, and a JD at the Thomas Jefferson School of Law in San Diego, California, where she excelled and received a coveted Am Jur Award. She is also the managing attorney of the Finz & Finz law firm.

My daughter Sandy and her husband Jerry have two children (my grandchildren), Brittany and Sean, who are twins. Brittany has a B.A. degree from Goucher College in Towson, Maryland, a unique and selective institution of higher learning which at one time was affiliated with Johns Hopkins University. She also has a JD degree from the University of Baltimore School of Law, and is presently employed by Universal Studios in Orlando, Florida.

Sean has a B.A. degree from Florida Gulf Coast University, and a JD degree from Loyola College of Law, New Orleans, Louisiana. He will soon be taking the national bar in Denver, Colorado, where he has already received several significant job offers from two of the largest law firms in Denver, the fastest growing city in the country.

Stuart and Cheri have two children (my grandchildren), Jackie and Brandon. Jackie has a B.A. degree from the University of Arizona in Tucson, and a JD degree from the Touro School of Law in New York, where she graduated with honors. She is an attorney and an associate with her father's law firm, Finz & Finz of Mineola and Manhattan, New York. She is married to Yoel Sarraf, a real estate specialist in Manhattan.

Brandon is a graduate of the business school of the University of Miami, Florida, with a B.B.A. degree, and an honor graduate with a JD degree from the Georgetown Law School in Washington, D.C. Recruited by fifteen Wall Street firms, he selected the Wall Street firm of Debevoise & Plimpton, and will specialize in corporate reorganization, and mergers and acquisitions. He was admitted to the Bar on December 7, 2016.

I have great pride in my family, hoping that to some extent the love and support Pearl and I gave to our children, their spouses, and to our grandchildren, in some small measure assisted their journey along a future path to success and happiness. But most of all, I am proudest of Pearl, my beloved wife who I will continue to love, cherish, and miss for the rest of my life.

Our wedding photo taken on December 26, 1948.

Certificate of Marriage

Leonard Leigh Finz and *Pearl Karen Sherman* were United in Marriage in *New York* on the *26th* day of *December* 1948 according to the laws of the State of *New York* and in accordance with the customs of Israel

Our certificate of marriage dated December 26, 1948.

Mrs. Bessie Sherman
Mr. and Mrs. Samuel S. Finz
request the honour of your presence
at the marriage of their children

Pearl
to
Leonard

on Sunday, the twenty-sixth of December
Nineteen hundred and forty-eight
at one o'clock in the afternoon

Cocoanut Grove
Park Central Hotel
Seventh Avenue and Fifty-fifth Street
New York City

Ceremony at one-thirty

Our wedding invitation noting December 26, 1948 as the date, and The Park Central Hotel in New York City as the place.

1952, with Pearl in Shreveport, LA, where I was the featured performer at the Stork Club, early in my entertainment career.

In Las Vegas, Nevada, circa 1980's.

With Pearl at a supper club in San Diego, CA, circa 1990's.

My daughter Sandy, and
son- in-law, Jerry Parker.

Jerry, Sean, Sandy and Brittany.
The Italian Alps are in the background.

Sandy and Jerry toasting their anniversary.

With my daughter, Sandy, in front of the
Wynn Hotel in Las Vegas, Nevada, where
the family celebrated my 90th birthday.

Our daughter Sandy and Pearl.

Sandy, Pearl, and Cheri, our daughter-in-law.

My grandson Sean, son-in-law Jerry, daughter Sandy, and granddaughter Brittany. I am in the background.

My son Stuart, and daughter, Sandy at a family gathering.

I'm seated next to Pearl. Our grandchildren, Sean, Brittany, Jackie, Brandon, are in the rear.

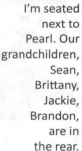

It's a happy birthday, with Sandy, Jerry, and Cheri, seated in front. Pearl and Stu are in the rear.

My son Stuart, and daughter Sandy, as young children. I am in the middle of them and Pearl is behind us.

With my daughter Sandy, both of us wearing cowboy hats. We are near Sandy's and Jerry's 400 acre ranch outside of Aspen, Colorado.

Our grandchildren, Brandon, Jackie, Brittany, and Sean.

With Sandy at an Aspen, Colorado July 4, 2016 celebration. A tall Uncle Sam is in the background.

Our daughter-in-law Cheri with our son Stuart.

Cheri and Pearl seated. Brandon and Jackie in background. Stuart is kneeling next to Pearl.

Our daughter-in-law Cheri, and our son Stuart, on a lounge in Naples, Florida.

With my grandson Sean, upon his graduation from Loyola College of Law in New Orleans, LA, on May 21, 2016.

With my son Stuart in the cockpit of his new 53-foot cabin cruiser. 2016

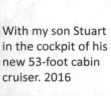

Sean in his cap and gown, holding his law school graduation book. May 21, 2016.

With my grandson, Sean. 2016.

With my granddaughter, Brittany. 2016.

My granddaughter, Brittany. 2015.

My granddaughters, Jackie and Brittany. 2014

My granddaughter, Brittany dressed for a wedding. 2015.

Equestrian rider Brittany, on her horse, "Uno". My daughter Sandy, my wife Pearl, and my grandson Sean, looking on.

My granddaughter Jackie with her husband Yoel, my-grandson-in-law. 2014.

My grandson Brandon, and my granddaughter, Jackie. 2013.

Springtime in Manhasset, New York. 2013.

With Sheba, Sandy and Jerry's dog,
in front of my home. 2012.

With my grandson, Brandon, upon his graduation
from Georgetown Law School in Washington D.C.,
on May 22, 2016.

My grandson Brandon upon his
graduation from Georgetown Law School,
Washington, D.C., on May 22, 2016.

With my mother
circa 1960's.

With my father, wearing my army
overseas cap, during my first
furlough during WWII. 1943.

With my older brother
Al in the center, and
my eldest brother
Bob, at the right end.
Circa late 1970's.

With my brother-in-law Paul, my sister Mollie, my mom, my
sister-in-law Maddy, my brother Bob, and my sister-in-law,
Bea, my brother Al's wife. I am at the far left. Circa 1960s.

With Pearl in our
Little Neck, NY, study.
Circa 1960's.

I am seated in an antique African
chair in the Los Angeles home of
one of our collector friends.

With Pearl, and the family celebrating my 90th birthday at the "Sinatra" restaurant in the Wynn Hotel, Las Vegas, Nevada, 2014.

My daughter Sandy, my son Stuart (on the extreme left) together with their friends in a campaign to raise money for Cerebral Palsy. 1965.

With my son Stuart after a set of tennis in San Diego, CA, where he was attending law school.

My daughter Sandy, and son-in-law Jerry. Circa 1980's.

With my son-in-law Jerry, Brittany, my wife Pearl, my daughter Sandy, and Sean. I am at the extreme right.

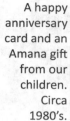

With Pearl in a restaurant at Lake Tahoe, NV. Circa 1980's.

My daughter Sandy and Pearl, in a casual moment, with Sheba on Pearls lap.

Here with my granddaughter Jackie celebrating my 92nd birthday. 2016.

Here with Jackie to my right, her husband Yoel to my left, and my grandson Brandon to Yoel's left. My son Stuart and my daughter in law Cheri are in the background. 2016.

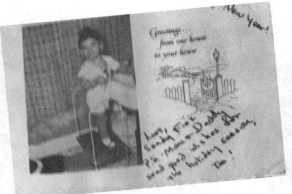

A holiday card with the pictures of
our daughter Sandy, and son Stuart. 1957.

I am looking over the shoulder of
my son Stuart in his law office.

I am discussing a legal point with my son Stuart.

Our daughter Sandy,
and son Stuart.

Sandy at the piano in our home,
as Stuart, Pearl and I watch and listen.

With my late wife Pearl during our 66th wedding anniversary on December 26, 2014.
In all, we were married for 67 ½ years.

I BECOME A PUBLISHED AUTHOR
OF FICTION THRILLERS

Finz' next chapter to storied career

Leonard Finz used his experiences as a soldier, entertainer and state Supreme Court justice in writing his three novels.

Having hit the age of 80, the time had come for me to leave the battleground of the courtroom, but the energy was still there. If possible, I had to ensure that my brain, involved in so many fierce litigation combats, did not turn into mush. To protect against such a cerebral decline, I decided to become an author of thriller novels. In that posture I could live vicariously through fictional characters and hopefully keep my active brain cells from turning into oatmeal.

Each day, I would set aside time to write another chapter of a thriller novel I had been working on. By happenstance, a neighbor and friend, Mike Hirsch, had a publishing company and large printing plant in Naples, Florida. At one of the dinner parties attended by Mike, his wife, Pearl, and I, it was mentioned casually how I was spending my free time. I informed Mike that I was writing a second thriller novel. The first one, "Arrowhead", had already been published by "Publish America", whose plant was in Maryland.

The end result was that Mike published my second novel, "The Paragon Conspiracy", and my third, "Reservation to Kill". All three published novels had been accepted by Amazon.com, Barnes and Noble, and other book sellers. In fact, all three titles with their book covers displayed on their websites are purchased even to this day. My interest has not been in royalties received (all go to charities anyway) but in trying to keep my brain busy enough so that it could not complain that it was being ignored.

Although none of my novels ever made the top ten best seller list, several did from time to time fall within the top 100. And considering that there are more than six million titles out there, having come within the "100" range was not too shabby for someone at my stage. But losing my loving wife in May of 2016 after 67 years of a wonderful marriage has had a significant effect upon my desire to write another novel. The scripting of this memoir however, is a palliative that has energized a dormant wish to

reveal some of the more significant events of my 92 years spent on this earth. It also serves as a much-needed therapeutic crutch during this most difficult period of my life.

With it all, and despite some renewed interest in writing, it still does not make for the greatest day of my life.

BACK TO WORLD WAR II

Having been transferred to a U. S. Army band in 1944 was a joy and a very cushy job. We'd play revile in the morning, go back to sleep and lounge around until summoned for a parade or field marching music for the GI's in training. At 5pm, we would line up in front of the flag (called retreat) and play the national anthem as it was lowered and folded military style. After retreat we would move quickly back to our barracks and within minutes would  be on our way to town where we would probably stay out all night. What would follow would be the good times young soldiers usually sought.

Answerable only to my Bandmaster (a Warrant Officer), and a real prince of a guy, it is what we then called, "Being in the Army, really?" I could have remained with that enviable assignment but somehow I didn't want to tell my future wife, kids, and grandchildren, that I spent the war playing clarinet and saxophone at dances and on the parade grounds when I was in the army. There was a World War going on and I felt it was my duty to become an active part of it.

MY APPLYING TO FIELD ARTILLERY
OFFICERS CANDIDATE SCHOOL (OCS)

Employing the proper protocol, I informed my Bandmaster that I wished to apply to Officers Candidate School and that I wanted his blessing. In response, he said, "Lenny, you've got the best thing going right here in the band. You could stay stateside throughout the war. I want you to know that if you're accepted into OCS, you'll be sent overseas right away and into battle. Is that what you really want?" My answer to him was a quick one. "Yes, I know what the probabilities are. But I must become a real part of our war. I feel it's my duty." With that, I applied to Officers Candidate School in the Field Artillery knowing if I was accepted and passed the four- month intensive course, I would be sent overseas and into combat.

A month after submitting my application through army channels, I received notice to report for an entrance intelligence test. Within a few weeks I received word that I passed the I.Q. requirements and that my name would be placed on a wait list since there were no opening slots at the time. That was the summer of 1944, when I was nineteen years of age. I received no further word for months despite my many inquiries regarding my status.

In the Fall of 1944, the Battle of the Bulge was exploding. Our soldiers suffered tremendous losses including many field artillery officers killed in action.

It was December 20, 1944, when I was suddenly called into the Bandmaster's office. He had just received orders for me from Washington. I was to report to the Field Artillery Officers Candidate School (OCS) in Fort Sill, Oklahoma, on December 31, 1944, as a member of class 133. I was also given a furlough to return home before reporting to Fort Sill. My emotions were mixed—sad that I would be leaving my buddies in the Army band with whom I had become so close, but exhilarated that I would soon be a candidate at OCS. When the news was given to my buddies in the band, they threw me a big party with all the good wishes along with it. I remember packing up my personal belongings in a barrack's bag and saying goodbye between many tears as I left the camp. By this time, we had already been transferred from Camp Pendleton in Virginia Beach, Virginia, to Camp Chafee, Arkansas.

Although being accepted into OCS was great news, it still was not the greatest day of my life.

MY REPORTING TO OCS AT FORT SILL, OKLAHOMA

I went on furlough and spent time with my mother, father, older brothers Bob and Al, and my sister Mollie, who I had not seen in over a year. At the end of my furlough I said a tearful goodbye to my family. I wasn't quite sure that if I ever made it through OCS and went into battle that I would ever see them again.

On December 31, 1944, I reported to Fort Sill, Oklahoma, presented my orders, was assigned to a barracks and a bunk, outfitted, and received a special ID nameplate that read, "Officer Candidate Leonard Finz". Although January 1st was New Year's Day, the lieutenant in charge of class 133 (called the "tach officer"—an abbreviation of "technical officer"), sent out a message that although the official four-month course would not begin until January 2nd, the members of class 133, all one hundred of us, were directed to line up in formation on January 1st, at 0800 hours (8am).

The next morning, we were marched to the parade grounds for a morning exercise drill. The first exercise was one in which each candidate individually was required to run one hundred yards, pick up a baton on the ground and run back as fast as he could. Those first called, made the run and did it almost effortlessly. The ones that followed were equally good. After all, they all came directly from line outfits, many of whom were battle-scarred first sergeants, master sergeants, tech sergeants, etc. I looked at them in awe. They had been actively involved in the war coming from the deadly battlefields of France, Italy, Germany, and the Pacific. By sharp contrast, I was a lowly private first class, the only PFC in the entire group. The only battlefield I ever saw was on a movie screen. For most of my army life I was a sax and clarinet player coming from a very soft and cushy job in an army band, stateside.

It then became my turn. I huffed and puffed as I ran since I was completely out of shape considering the easy and leisurely lifestyle I came from. I ran the hundred yards, reached down to pick up the baton, turned around and started to run back. Suddenly, I felt dizzy and nauseous and before I even reached the end of the run, had to stop, bent over and vomited with such force that I thought that my gut was part of the contents. With that exhibition I knew I would be bounced from the class even before I officially started it. The fact is, I was in lousy shape competing with ninety-nine other strong and seasoned army warriors. Although the tach officer said nothing, I had an ominous feeling I would be dropped from the class when we returned to the barracks. Somehow, I was not.

Although I was not called to task by the tach officer, it was not one of the greatest days of my life.

OFFICERS CANDIDATE SCHOOL
AND ITS PROSPECTS

Our class started with a roster of one hundred, most of whom were hardened fighters who reported to Fort Sill directly from the front. Each day however, a member of the class would usually be called into the tach officer's office. It was always bad news. "You're being dropped." There was never a reason given and no appeal from the decision. After four months of the most rigorous West Point-like training there was a graduation ceremony. Of the original one hundred candidates, only thirty-two eventually made the grade. From the start, I was always uncertain whether I would be one who would make it.

F**K YOUR BUDDY WEEK

There were so many difficult hurdles that an officer candidate had to jump over without falling on his face, that it almost became impossible to define each one with any degree of exactitude. The four-month course was so physically and mentally demanding, as to push human endurance to its  extreme limits. But there is one I will describe that falls somewhere between a physical and mental challenge. It played out like this...

At the end of the first rigorous month of the course there was what was called, "F**k your buddy week." Each of the officer candidates received a sheet containing the names of each member of the class in alphabetical order. It also contained a lined grid next to each name with eleven columns. Thus, as you read across the sheet it would start with the name of the candidate followed by eleven blank columns each with its own heading at the top of the column. These were the headings: Leadership; Courage; Intelligence; Confidence; Discipline; Mental Fitness; Physical Fitness; Responsibility; Performance Under Pressure; Quick Decisions; and, Comradery.

Assuming there were fifty named candidates at the time, it was now our duty to attach a number to each category as to where in our judgement we thought the candidate stood in the overall class rating. Thus, the best candidate could conceivably receive a "1" in all columns or any other number from "1" to "50." Conversely, the worst considered candidate would receive a "50" or a different rating in any of the columns.

We learned that the tach officer used our ratings to make his own determination as to how each class member rated the other and who was rated the best and proceeding down to the worst in the class. If a candidate attached good numbers to a friend based upon his relationship but who received poor numbers from the others, it would reflect negatively upon the one reporting, thereby demonstrating a lack of good judgement that could even be the basis of his being dropped. Consequently, even if he was your best friend you had to rate him honestly. If he was the worst student, he should receive a "50" in a number of the columns. That is how the process got its name, "F**k your buddy week".

This tough procedure was repeated at the end of each month and was always one of the most difficult and personal burdens we had to go through when, "F**k your buddy week" was with us again.

The class ratings of each candidate in the 11 categories would be a most significant factor the tach officer employed, combined with class performance and his own one-on-one appraisals. It was amazing and sad to see the many candidates who were shown the door after each dreaded, "F**k your buddy week" occurred. It was just another rigid device used in an already extremely challenging and competitive course to whittle away those candidates who were viewed as not being of sufficient officer material to lead soldiers in combat against the enemy.

MY FINAL OCS EXAM ON "KILLER MOUNTAIN"

Those of us who survived being axed from the class had to scale the wall of the final hurdle in the last week of the four-month course. We had to pass the test on "Killer Mountain", having received its name since a candidate who flunked the final exam would be dropped from the class. Thus, the mountain could be the "killer" of one's hopes of ever becoming an officer in the army. To put it in understandable terms, each candidate perched on the mountain situated a few miles from Fort Sill, after being designated a target thousands of yards in front, would have to direct cannon fire that would destroy the target through commands radioed to the artillery batteries hundreds of yards behind our position. We would be graded upon speed and accuracy. The failure of one or the other could end our candidacy as officers in the field artillery.

With the above as a backdrop, these are the details...

At 0700 (7am), our class (what remained of it) was marched to army trucks a quarter of a mile away. Once inside, we were driven through rugged country toward one of the high mountains a few miles from Fort

Sill. When the trucks reached their destination, we dismounted. The heavy rains of the night before and into the morning hours brought so much mud that the muck was above our army boots and well over our leggings. We were directed to another mud-filled area several hundred yards above where the trucks had stopped.

There, we were instructed by our tach officer (he was accompanied by two other field artillery officers at the time) to remain in that holding area while a candidate would be called out who would then be put to his test. Intentionally, we were kept from observing the process thereby removing any advantage we might have gained in watching a candidate go through his final exam on, "Killer Mountain".

As each candidate was called up, we would hear cannon shots and shells swishing with thunderous sounds, like a freight train above us, heading hopefully toward the target selected by the tach officer. The candidates called before me didn't know if they had passed the test since no information was being released.

In due time I heard the call, "Candidate Finz, front and center." It was now my turn. I trudged through the mud with my large binoculars in hand and was escorted to the top of "Killer Mountain".

In actual combat, a field artillery officer would be in the front lines ahead of the infantry (sometimes even in enemy territory) with the artillery batteries lined up behind the foot soldiers. It would then be the artillery officer's duty to select the target, estimate its distance from the cannon batteries, determine its straight or lateral position, and determine whether it was a stationary target such as a farm house where enemy machine gun fire was coming from, or a moving target such as tanks, armored vehicles or even foot soldiers. To accomplish this, geometric angles would have to be plotted.

All components would be factored into commands radioed to the gun batteries in the rear. It was imperative therefore that the target (assuming it was a stationary one such as a farm house) be surrounded by single cannon shots that would be seen in the distance as a puff of smoke. It would be necessary to give commands that would discharge individual cannon shells to the north, south, east, and west of the target. Accomplishing that is what in field artillery jargon is called a "bracket".

Once a bracket is accomplished by single cannon shots, the field artillery officer would then radio a command to, "Fire for effect." With that order, the entire gun battery would fire its cannons with the expectation that the target selected by the artillery officer would be destroyed. Time and accuracy were essential in order to take out the target before the enemy could cause further casualties to our side.

MY TARGET IS THAT FARM HOUSE
WITH THE BROWN ROOF

With the previous segment as a back-drop, I was told my target was, "That small farm house with the brown roof." The exam clock started to run. I could see no farm house with my naked eye. Using my high-powered binocs, I was able to make out a small structure that appeared to have a brown roof.

My next step (as the clock was running), was to quickly estimate its distance from the gun batteries behind me. Such a numeral would create a geometric angle that would give me a calibrated number to direct the elevation of the barrel of the cannon. A decreased number would direct the gunnery squad to lower the barrel, in which case the shell would travel further. An elevated barrel would form an arc so that the shell would travel a shorter distance. The next step was to determine the target's lateral position since the command had to be accurate enough so that the shell would explode to the east or west of the target, thereby forming the east or west edge of the bracket. That number would be radioed to the battery commander in the rear with the order to, "Fire one." Within a second I heard the swishing sound overhead as I placed my binocs to my eyes hoping to see a puff of smoke either slightly north or south of the farm house. And there it was. The puff of smoke was north of the target. I now had to readjust the number hoping that the next puff would be to the south of the farm house, and it was.

But my laterals were off. I quickly adjusted my numbers and radioed the new laterals praying that the puff of smoke would be to the east or west of the farm house. Fortunately, it was. At the end, I had bracketed the target and sent out my commands to the battery commander behind my position: "Battery adjust, shell HE, fuse quick, elevation, base deflection right, fire for effect." The signals radioed were immediately relayed to the gunnery squad leaders. Within seconds it sounded as if the sky had exploded as each cannon, all twenty of them, was fired. Looking through my binoculars, the farm house had been destroyed. At that point the tach officer gave me those reassuring words, "Nice job."

I left, "Killer Mountain" reasonably sure I would not be added to its list of victims. Three other officer candidates were not as fortunate. My time for graduation and commission as a Second Lieutenant was finally in sight but not there yet.

MY ASSIGNMENT TO THE FIRST ASSAULT WAVE ON JAPAN

At the end of OCS, orders soon came down to report to Fort Ord, California, for training in Japanese. Each day during a one-month period we trained climbing down the netting of a troop ship and into small landing crafts that would then quickly proceed to the beach where we would go through practice landings. This was in preparation for the assault on Japan. As a field artillery officer my assigned role was that of a Forward Observer. It was my job to be up front ahead of the infantry, to select an observation post and to radio the coordinates of Japanese targets to the artillery batteries lined up behind the infantry. I was to be part of the first attack force on Japan.

After a month of simulated attacks, I was ordered to Camp Anza in Los Angeles and directed onto a troop ship heading for the Pacific theatre, place unknown. On day one, the ocean swells were so violent as to cause the ship to list almost forty-five degrees from side to side for twenty-four hours straight. I was never so seasick in my life. Glued to my bunk, I was nauseous and dizzy, with such a violent headache that I thought I would die. By day four, the Pacific was much calmer. I learned for the first time that the G.I.s and officers, almost five thousand troops in all, were headed for Okinawa. I was also told I would be assigned to the 27th Infantry Division as a Field Artillery Forward Observer and again told I would be in the first assault wave hitting the Japanese beach.

On day thirty-two however, there was an announcement over the loud speaker that altered the lives of millions of G.I.s, and the world forever. It started with, "Now hear this, this is the Captain speaking, the United States

Air Force has dropped atomic bombs on Hiroshima and Nagasaki. Hear this. Japan has surrendered. The war is over." One had to be there to believe it. The shouts; screams; tears. We were soon informed that due to the war's end, our ship was being diverted to Tacloban, Leyte, in the Philippine Islands.

While there has been much honest debate whether the use of such catastrophic bombs was inhumane, thus casting the morality of the United States in its worst posture, there is general agreement that had we attacked the Japanese mainland as planned by General MacArthur, up to one million soldiers, marines, and navy personnel would have perished. There were 400,000 Japanese soldiers dug in, and hundreds of kamikaze planes waiting for our attack, ready to fight to the death.

The most recent book on the continuing controversy, is the detailed and incisive best seller, "Killing the Rising Sun," by Bill O'Reilly and Martin Dugard. In it, O'Reilly writes passionately about his father, a World War II Navy ensign who would have been part of the attack force upon Japan. "He firmly believed he would be killed if MacArthur's land invasion had come to fruition."

O'Reilly concludes with what is enormously profound, with which I identify so strongly to this day. "But for the young ensign and his present-day son, there is no debate, only a stark reality. Had the A-bombs not been used, you would very likely not be reading this book." To which, I add, being in the first wave of attack upon the Japanese shores as a field artillery forward observer, I would, in all probability, not have survived the assault.

There would be no future wife. No future children. No future grandchildren. No future whatsoever. Nothing but a tombstone. And taking the liberty of borrowing Mr. O'Reilly's poignant "stark reality" about his father, and transferring it to me, you would "not be reading this" memoir.

MILITARY COURT MARTIAL AND DEFENSE COUNSEL

In Leyte, with the war over, a combat field artillery officer was no longer needed. I was therefore assigned as the officer in charge of arranging transportation for the repatriation of the thousands of Filipinos who escaped their islands to avoid the invasion by the ruthless Japanese Imperial Army. After three or four months of that assignment, my commanding officer, a bird colonel, ordered me into his office. He sat me down and said, "Finz, there are over fifty G.I.s held prisoner in our guard house. They've been rotting there for months waiting for a court martial trial but there's only one officer on the island who's a lawyer in the Judge Advocate General's branch here in Leyte. He can only serve as a prosecutor. There's no other army lawyer in Leyte who can act as defense counsel for the prisoners awaiting trial. But under the manual, in the absence of a JAG lawyer any officer of any branch can be assigned as defense counsel. I want you, Finz, to be that defense counsel."

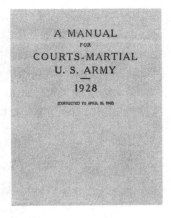

I was flabbergasted. My response was, "Sir, I'm only a high school graduate. I don't even have any college credit. Why me?" His answer was, "I've watched you carefully. I checked your work. You're solid and a good officer. I know I can count on you to do the right thing. I'd like you to volunteer for the job. Of course, you could say 'No' and I would certainly understand."

I answered, "If you're making that request of me sir, my answer is 'Yes'." Result? Orders came down and I was assigned as Defense Counsel, supplied with a jeep since I would have to travel deep into the jungles to search out witnesses. The danger as reported to me, was that my only protection from any Japanese soldiers who did not know the war was over, either hiding in caves or refusing to surrender would be my 45-caliber pistol. It was pretty heavy duty stuff for a twenty-year-old.

I read and studied the army court martial manual and visited the stockade every day, meeting with every one of the prisoners awaiting a court martial trial. I got to know them each by their first names. In fact, I was there so often that the MPs on duty would kid me and say they had a special cell reserved just for me so that I could sleep there and not have to go back home to my quarters each night.

In the next six months, I tried all the cases, over fifty of them, defending deserters, burglars, those charged with assault and other types of crimes committed by those G.I.s who had been locked up in the guard house for such an endless period of time. After a while I was almost able to quote the entire army courts martial manual from memory having studied it so much. In addition, it was imperative that I interview witnesses, many of whom lived in remote shacks in the Philippine jungles. It was indeed a most responsible, difficult, and life-risking assignment.

AN INVITATION TO THE
HIGH-RANKING OFFICER'S CLUB

Within the six-month period, I defended more than fifty G.I.s in individual court martial trials. I either received acquittals for most of them or had the others released for time already served. It was during this period that I was invited by my colonel to the high-ranking officer's club (majors, lieutenant colonels, and colonels). When I arrived, he told me to turn around with my back toward him. Suddenly, I felt slight pressure on my shoulders. Something was going on but I was in the dark as to what exactly was happening. A few minutes later he told me to turn around. As I did, he saluted me and said, "Congratulations First Lieutenant Finz upon your promotion." The high-ranking officers in attendance who had encircled us let out a loud round of applause. What I obviously felt was the colonel removing my second lieutenant's gold bars and replacing them with the silver first lieutenant's bars.

Facing me, the colonel said, "First Lieutenant Finz, not only did you earn the promotion through your exceptional work as defense counsel but I'm also recommending that you be decorated for distinguished service."

I never did receive the medal at the time, since my orders for departure from the Philippines back to the United States had already arrived.

Being promoted to first lieutenant at age twenty under all of the circumstances was quite an honor, but even that did not add up to the greatest day of my life.

MY DISCOVERY SIXTY YEARS LATER

I had completely forgotten what the colonel had said when he promoted me to first lieutenant, that he would recommend I be awarded a medal for distinguished service. It was now the year 2004, when I was clearing out papers that had accumulated in the closet of my home when I came across an envelope that contained some of my army personnel records and a copy of a memorandum sent by the Judge Advocate General, my commanding officer, to the Secretary of the Army regarding a decoration. What was not important to me at the time (I was more concerned with returning home to my family), suddenly at my age became of great meaning to me, sixty years later. As a result, I sent off a letter to my congressman, Gary Ackerman, setting out the particulars of my service as defense counsel, requesting that I be awarded, "The Army Commendation Medal", in keeping with the JAG officer's memo.

Within a short time, I received word he sent my letter to the Secretary of the Army to await a response. A week or two after that, I was informed that I would be decorated with The United States Army Commendation Medal at a formal ceremony to take place at the World War II Memorial in Washington D.C. with a full honor guard and high ranking army officials.

MY MEDAL DECORATION AT THE
WORLD WAR II MEMORIAL IN WASHINGTON, D.C.

On October 5, 2004, I appeared at the Capitol of the United States dressed in my army officer's uniform flanked by my family and friends. Together with Congressman Ackerman and his staff, we were driven to the World War II Memorial.

There, I was greeted with an honor guard and officers provided by the Secretary of the Army to participate in a formal ceremony. A lectern had already been set up together with several hundred chairs that were filled by friends and other veterans who were visiting the World War II Memorial. A United States flag encased in a beautiful oak wood triangular frame was presented to me, in addition to a certificate attesting that the flag had been flown over the Capitol of the United States for one full day in my honor.

Thereafter, Congressman Ackerman, in the presence of the honor guard with their flags flowing in the breeze and a team of riflemen, presented me with all of the medals I had earned and pinned the United States Army Commendation Medal onto my jacket. I received the medal for distinguished service and meritorious achievement in carrying out my duties as defense counsel. The certificate I received also contained language that through my service I had elevated the course of military justice in the United States. Following the ceremony, we were given personal tours of the Capitol and the House of Representatives which was in session. We then had lunch at a hotel with windows that faced the White House. The day was a tremendous honor and one I will never forget.

It brought back very special and nostalgic memories, but still was not the greatest day of my life.

MY RETURN FROM THE PHILIPPINES

Finally, the time came for me to leave the Philippines. From Leyte, I was transferred to Manila, where after a few days I was directed onto a troop ship that would take me back to the states and ultimately to my home and family. Within two weeks the ship was cutting water through the waves under the Golden Gate Bridge in San Francisco, California. I remember (and will never forget) walking down the gang plank and setting both feet on American soil. It was an indescribable feeling. I made it. I survived the war. I would soon be home. It all felt as if I was in the middle of some surrealistic experience.

Having orders in hand to report to Ft. Dix, New Jersey, where I would be processed for discharge from the army, I proceeded to a holding area for officers awaiting transportation to the nearest base. As I stood there with my Japanese Samurai sword given to me by one of the G.I. prisoners

I had defended in a court martial he had taken from a Japanese officer he captured (a sword I have to this day), in addition to all the gear I had stashed in a large barracks bag, I was blown away when I saw a familiar face several yards from me.

MY FORMER FIRST SERGEANT WILSON

"My God," it was Wilson, the Southern, bigoted, first sergeant who made my life so miserable as I was going through basic training as a private. He was still a first sergeant, a non-commissioned officer, but I was now an officer with the rank of first lieutenant.

Seeing him, I called out, "Hey you, Sergeant Wilson, front and center." He turned around quickly and responded to my waving him over. When standing two feet in front of me, he looked quizzical, unsure who I was. "Stand-up straight," I ordered. "Salute an officer, mister, yah hear?" I ordered. "Do you recognize me?" I asked with a snarl. He squinted and suddenly the light bulb turned on. Meekly, he said, "Yeah, you were in my outfit with the 46th," he retorted with obvious surprise in his voice.

"When you address an officer, you say, 'Sir', do you read me, mister?" I responded. "Yes, Sir" he answered grudgingly. "And get your gut in and chest out. Stand at attention when you address an officer." He followed my orders reluctantly.

I had never forgotten how cruel he was, particularly when he refused to give me my weekend pass because of some phony demerit during a Saturday morning inspection. I remember pleading that my mother was already on her way from New York to visit me, and his callous response, "Well now, isn't that tough s**t?" He turned and started to walk away. I ordered him back. "When you're dismissed, you salute an officer." He curled his upper lip and gave me a feint salute. I barked out, "Now, mister, you're dismissed." With scorn written all over his craggy face, he turned around and started to walk away. I shouted, "Hey Wilson, did you forget something?" With that, he threw me a mild salute and quickly disappeared.

By nature, I am not a vindictive person, but in Wilson's case I at least received some satisfaction. And as it is often said, "What goes around, comes around." The most recent Wilson experience made me feel real good. And as Jackie Gleason with his signature expression used to say, "How sweet it is." To that, my response is, "Ditto, Mr. G."

Miraculously, I also ran into my former Executive Officer Lt. Moore who was my protector from Wilson when I would call upon him to shield me. He was now Captain Moore, and recognized me immediately. I threw him a  sharp salute and felt so exhilarated in seeing him again. He returned it and followed it up with a manly hug. He was sincerely thrilled at my rank. We spoke of our service in the Pacific and mused over the times he saved me from Wilson's terror. I also told him about my graduating from OCS at the field artillery school in Fort Sill, Oklahoma.

Lt. Moore, now Captain Moore, was one of the most decent human beings I had ever met. Within a short while, our buses arrived, each of us boarding separate vehicles to be transported to different locations. We parted and I never saw him again. But dressing down my former first sergeant who qualified in every department as a miserable SOB and seeing my former executive officer who I admired and respected so much, were very special moments.

Amazingly, each had contributed elements to help shape my character but in far different ways. As for Wilson, I learned that tolerance and respect for one another would always overcome bullying and intimidation. Regarding Captain Moore, he reinforced my deep feeling for fair play, that human decency and the desire to come to the aid of one who needs it, are far greater attributes than stubborn indifference with its callous absence of conscience.

Although the surprising events I experienced after the ship landed were most rewarding ones, they still did not measure up to being the greatest day of my life.

THE GREATEST DAY OF MY LIFE

At this point the reader might ask impatiently, "So, what was the greatest day of your life?" The answer compels me to return to my candidacy at the Fort Sill, Officers Candidate School. The four-month course was an unbelievably enormous experience. It matched West Point training in every respect, from leadership, to the breaking down of a jeep's engine, to geometry, but most of all, to the special pride of being a candidate training to become an army field artillery officer. I remember so clearly the last three days prior to graduation. From the original 100 candidates in the class, we were now down to 33. But graduating was still no certainty.

Graduation was scheduled to be held on Saturday, May 6, 1945. On Thursday, we received officers' uniforms having been outfitted a week earlier. But even that was no guaranty that I would not be called into the tach office and bounced. In fact, when Saturday morning did arrive, another candidate was suddenly dropped, reducing the class number to 32.

On Saturday morning, I put on my officer's uniform absent the gold bars. In the early morning hours, the 32 remaining candidates in the class stood in rigid formation. When ordered, we marched with military precision to the post chapel a short distance away. Once inside, we received the order to sit down. High ranking officers were already on the stage in front. Soon, a brigadier general made some opening remarks. Within minutes, individual names were sounded out in alphabetical order.

At the sound of his name, the candidate marched up to the stage, was pinned with gold lieutenant bars, and exchanged military salutes. I had the terrifying thought that at any moment the tach officer would summon me to his office. While in a trance and harboring such a dire possibility, I suddenly heard the general call out from the stage, "Officer Candidate Finz, front and center." I rose from my seat, made a sharp right turn into the isle and marched crisply to the stage. With a slight smile, the general pinned gold bars onto my dress jacket epaulets while simultaneously saying, "Congratulations Lieutenant Finz." He saluted me and I returned it as if I was in a dream. I couldn't believe I made it.

When the ceremony was over, we all euphorically walked out of the chapel. *"Was this really happening?"* I kept thinking to myself. Just moments before I was one stripe above a private, a PFC, a sax and clarinet player who came from an army band, who competed with the bravest battle scarred soldiers I had ever met, and now at age 20, commissioned a second lieutenant in the army of the United States of America. The chills I felt were unbelievably priceless, made even more so when I left the chapel and received my first salute from a soldier in the Women's Army Corps (WAC). She had that coy smile knowing those gold bars were just pinned on me. Returning it with a telling wink, I responded by saluting her with a crisp military flair.

It all seemed so surrealistic and indeed even at the age of 92 I can say what I have always felt in my heart for the past 72 years, that being commissioned a second lieutenant in the army of my beloved country was indeed <u>the greatest day of my life</u>.

There, I finally said it. But to stop here would be a great disservice to the many who are still hoping to find their greatest day. To those of you I say, without preaching and with all humility, that somewhere within your own wondrous experiences lies the greatest day of <u>your</u> life. If that as yet has not arrived, then follow the masterful poetry of Robert Browning, one of the greatest bards of the 19th Century whose magical words created this immortal inspirational message: To gain what is good but seems unattainable, your "reach should exceed" your "grasp." It is also in that spirit that an anonymous author wrote, "To achieve anything worthwhile, one should attempt even those things that may appear to be impossible."

So take that risk and extra step toward your own magical goal and you too may come upon <u>your</u> greatest day. I did just that and discovered what will always be the greatest day of <u>my</u> life.

This was taken of the remaining 33 officer candidates on May 4, 1945, two days prior to graduation. On graduation day, May 6, 1945, an additional candidate was dropped from the class, reducing the number to 32. I appear in the circle. The tach officer is in the first row, extreme right.

I am holding a Japanese Samurai sword, and wearing a jungle helmet. The sword was gifted to me by one of the G.I.'s I defended who was found to be, "Not guilty."

In the Philippines.

The medal ceremony program held at the WWII Memorial
in Washington, D.C. on October 5, 2004.

Congressman Gary L. Ackerman
pinning medals onto my uniform jacket.

Army veteran waits 58 years for medals

By JOEL ESKOVITZ
eskovitzj@shns.com

WASHINGTON — The medals didn't mean that much to 22-year-old Leonard Finz, a New Yorker who had opted to leave the somewhat cushy job of entertaining the troops to become a soldier.

It was 1946, and he had just been discharged from the Army, returning home from an unexpected assignment for someone with no legal training and only a high-school degree: defense counsel for soldiers accused of crimes in the Philippines. Included in the paperwork he received was a letter to his superior officer from the

See **MEDALS**, Page **10A**

Leonard Finz salutes the audience at the World War II Memorial during an awards ceremony in honor of his service.
Scripps Howard News Service

This is the story and photograph that appeared on the front page of a Script Howard newspaper.

I am standing at attention with Congressman Ackerman prior to the playing of the National Anthem.

The Honor Guard at the medal ceremony.

The Honor Guard in salute formation at the medal ceremony held at the World War II Memorial in Washington, D.C.

Members of the military preparing for the medal ceremony.

My daughter Sandy, son Stuart, and me in the middle, on the day of the medal ceremony held at the World War II Memorial in Washington, D.C. The Washington Monument is in the background.

Members of the family, friends, and visitors in the audience at the World War II Memorial, in honor of my medal ceremony.

I am kneeling to Pearl, and holding her hand in a very proud moment.

With my family, friends, and Congressman Ackerman. The Capitol dome is in background.

This is the actual American flag that was flown in my honor atop the Capitol building for one full day. It was thereafter presented to me at the medal ceremony held at the WWII Memorial.

THE FLAG
OF THE
UNITED STATES
OF AMERICA

This is to certify that the accompanying flag was flown over the United States Capitol on August 19, 2004, at the request of the Honorable Gary L. Ackerman, Member of Congress.

This flag was flown for Judge Leonard Finz, who has distinguished himself in meritorious service from November 13, 1945 to April 18, 1946, in Tacloban Leyte and will be presented with the Army Commendation Medal on October 5, 2004.

Alan M. Hantman, FAIA
Ar

2004-063946-001

This is the certificate of the architect of the Capitol certifying that the American flag was flown in my honor for "distinguished" and "meritorious service" performed in Leyte, Philippines.

Congressman Ackerman presenting me with the American flag that was flown in my honor atop the Capitol of the United States.

The American flag and medals presented to me in a triangular oak wood case.

Congressman Ackerman with me waving, as he displays the official Army Commendation Award certificate. The Honor Guard is in the background.

An army Lt. Colonel holds the plate of medals as Congressman Ackerman selects the next medal to be pinned onto my uniform jacket. The Honor Guard is in the background.

Congressman Ackerman addressing the audience at my medal ceremony held at the WWII Memorial in Washington, D.C.

A group picture with Congressman Ackerman. I am holding Pearl's hand, surrounded by our grandchildren, Brandon, Sean, Jackie, and Brittany. The Honor Guard is in the background.

My older brother Bob speaking to the audience about me. He was 8 years my senior, and no longer with us.

I am in deep thought, remembering my army buddies who are no longer with us.

I am in front of the United States Capitol.

NEW YORK UNIVERSITY
A private university in the public service

School of Law

40 WASHINGTON SQUARE SOUTH, NEW YORK, N.Y. 10012-1099
TELEPHONE: (212) 998-6000
FACSIMILE: (212) 995-3150
E-MAIL: richard.revesz@nyu.edu

Richard L. Revesz
Dean and Lawrence King Professor of Law

October 14, 2004

The Honorable Leonard L. Finz
19 Meadow Lane
Manhassett, NY 11030-3932

Dear Judge Finz:

I just learned of your recent honor in Washington D.C. for your World War II service. Congratulations for this terrific recognition of your wonderful work defending your fellow soldiers.

Judge Finz, I am always delighted to see a member of our community receive an acknowledgement that reflects such great accomplishment and dedication to his country and to the cause of justice. Your achievements honor New York University School of Law and serve as a terrific example for our students.

My very best wishes to you for continued success in all your endeavors. I look forward to meeting and renewing my acquaintance with all of the Law School's remarkable graduates and friends each year – you have made it truly rewarding to serve as dean of this institution. I hope you will have a chance to come and visit us soon for an alumni event, or to stop by and have a look at the newly renovated Vanderbilt Hall, as well as our recently completed facility, Furman Hall. It would be a great pleasure to have you back at Washington Square!

Warm regards,

Richard Revesz

RR/ao

A letter from Richard Revesz, Dean of my alma mater, the New York University School of Law.

DEPARTMENT OF THE ARMY

THIS IS TO CERTIFY THAT THE SECRETARY OF THE ARMY HAS AWARDED

THE ARMY COMMENDATION MEDAL

TO LEONARD L. FINZ
(THEN FIRST LIEUTENANT, FIELD ARTILLERY, ARMY OF THE UNITED STATES)

FOR distinguishing himself by meritorious service from 13 November 1945 to 18 April 1946, in Tacloban, Leyte, while assigned to the 668th Medium Port Company, Base K. Lieutenant Finz's outstanding contribution to military justice while assigned as a defense counsel on military court martials is in keeping with the highest standards of the military service and reflects great credit upon himself, his unit, and the Army of the United States.

THIS 6TH DAY OF AUGUST 2004

Permanent Orders Number 174-61 of 22 June 2004
U.S. Army Human Resources Command
Alexandria, VA 22332-0471

THE ADJUTANT GENERAL

DA FORM 4980-14, NOV 97

This is the official certificate of The Army Commendation Medal
issued by the Secretary of the Army.

My WWII Veteran's cap.

File No.			Subject:	
From	To	Date	Remarks:	
JA	CO 668 Med Port	28 April 1946		

1. I wish to call to your attention the very meritorious work being done by 1st Lt. Leonard Finz.

2. On 13 Nov 1945 he was appointed Assistant Defense Counsel for a Base K Special Courts Martial. About a month later he was appointed DC of the Court. He is not a lawyer and had no previous legal experience. Despite this he took a great interest in his assignment and set about to learn legal procedure in order that he might better represent the accused. On his own time he studied the Manual of Courts Martial and TM 27-255 and other legal publications that might furnish him legal information that he needed as Defense Counsel. He took a personal interest in each case assigned to him. He went to the Stockade as often as necessary to interview accused who were in confinement. He drove many miles over the Island of Leyte to interview witnesses. He found and presented to the Court all the evidence that could be adduced in favor of the accused. He worked hard on each case and each accused left the court feeling that he had had a fair trial and that his Counsel had taken a sincere interest in his welfare. Lt. Finz showed great initiative perseverance and aggressiveness in his work. He is at present DC on two Base K Special Courts and has tried approximately 50 cases. Each case has taken a lot of his personal time. His fine work has made the Courts function better and has been a distinct contribution to Military Justice at Base K. His work is outstanding and highly appreciated by this Office If you care to have him Officially commended I will be glad to furnish this information in proper form. This is entirely unsolicited by Lt. Finz.

J. E. KUNTZ
Captain, TC
Staff Judge Advocate

This is the memorandum issued by the Staff Judge Advocate
dated "28 April 1946" that formed the basis of my army decoration.

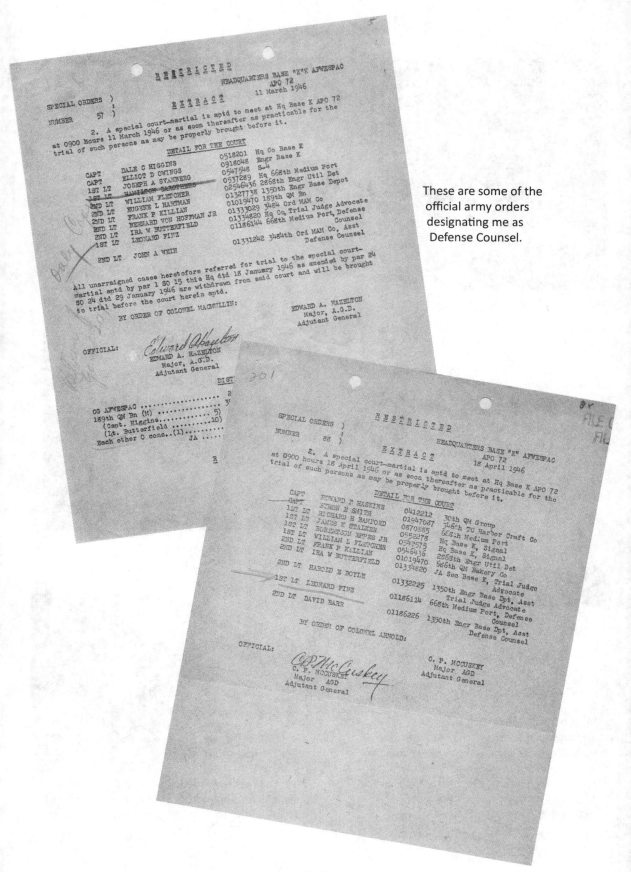

These are some of the official army orders designating me as Defense Counsel.

A cave in the Philippine jungles where Japanese hid and refused to surrender, a danger I faced when trying to locate witnesses in my role as defense counsel.

A typical Philippine jungle.

This is the 45 type caliber side arm that was my only protection when I went into the small villages of Leyte to seek out witnesses on behalf of the army soldiers I was assigned to defend at court martial trials. Japanese enemy snipers were still on the island, hiding in the jungles, or in caves.

This is the open-type Jeep I used to drive through dangerous terrain in order to search out witnesses who were in the small villages of Leyte, Philippines.

242

I am seated in a Filipino home in Tacloban, Leyte, having been invited as a "guest of honor." I am surrounded by Filipinos, several of whom were related to some of the G.I.'s I defended and who were married to Filipino girls. By honoring me in such a manner, they were expressing gratitude on behalf of my assisting the American soldiers in the guard house who had become members of their families.

This is a hand carved name plate gifted to me by a grateful Filipino family as a result of my service as Defense Counsel.

This is a Samurai sword gifted to me by a grateful G.I. I defended and who was acquitted. The sword had been taken from a Japanese officer he had captured.

HOME AT LAST

My mother is waiting for me to arrive from
the Philippines. There is a large American
flag and a lightbulb-framed sign that reads,

"WELCOME HOME LEONARD"

(The sign was put together by my father)

THE NATIONAL WORLD WAR II MUSEUM

I recently visited the National WWII Museum located in New Orleans. Seeing a 45 minute, spell-binding 4D movie produced and narrated by the Hollywood legend, Tom Hanks, was inspirational just by itself. But then add extraordinary World War II history dramatically displayed throughout the museum, and it all takes you on a magical journey through one of the most challenging and perilous chapters of our nation's 241 years of freedom.

The museum was founded by two visionaries, Gordon H. "Nick" Mueller, Ph.D., and the late professor of history, Steven E. Ambrose, who recognized the need to perpetuate the memory of those who served in uniform during World War II. Tom Hanks serves as the museum's Honorary Chair of its present Capital Campaign. Add to that, the words of Tom Brokaw, the famed author of, "The Greatest Generation": "Today, this generation is passing into the night. Their legacy is the legacy of freedom. It is our legacy. One that we should never take for granted... They came of age during the Great Depression and the Second World War and went on to build modern America – men and women whose everyday lives of duty, honor, achievement and courage gave us the world we have today."

Upwards of 30 million Americans have had a parent, grandparent, or close relative who served in World War II. As a WWII veteran, 95% of whom are no longer with us, my visit to the museum has added a further emotional dimension to my life, one I will carry with great pride forever. What I saw, was beyond belief. What I came away with, I will never forget.